THE VIEWER'S
TELEVISION BOOK

THE VIEWER'S TELEVISION BOOK

A Personal Guide
to Understanding Television
and Its Influence

Dr. Stanley J. Baran

PENRITH PUBLISHING COMPANY
CLEVELAND, OHIO

Library of Congress Catalog Card No. 80-81369
ISBN—0-936522-00-3

PENRITH PUBLISHING COMPANY
P.O. Box 18070   Cleveland Heights, Ohio 44118

To my students,
who challenge my ideas
as I try to challenge theirs.

ABOUT THE AUTHOR

Dr. Stanley J. Baran is an Associate Professor of Radio-Television-Film at the University of Texas at Austin. He earned his Ph. D. in Mass Communication Research at the University of Massachusetts in 1973. He has written over forty articles, book chapters, monographs, and books on the effects of mass communication. He has won the Teaching Excellence Award at the University of Texas, been nominated for an Emmy by the Cleveland Chapter of the National Academy of Television Arts and Sciences, and has done extensive grant work for broadcasters, foundations, and government agencies.

CONTENTS

THE VIEWER'S
TELEVISION BOOK

CHAPTER 1

INTRODUCTION

Pamela Kanagawa, 17, told police Steven T. Foerstel forced the family to watch television with him all morning.

> —From a UPI wire story reporting the knife-point holding of the Kanagawa family in Jefferson City, Missouri by an escaped convicted rapist, July, 1979.

Once, when talking to a PTA group, I met a woman who blamed television for killing her pet gerbil, Danny (Danny had eaten through the television's cord and was electrocuted). Leslie Van Houten, one of Charles Manson's Tate-LaBianca murder accomplices, accused television of instigating her involvement in those seven 1969 murders. Another Manson Family member, Brenda McCann, was more specific. She had become, she said, what "Gunsmoke," "The FBI," "Have Gun Will Travel," and "Combat" had made her become. A researcher at Stanford University claims to have demonstrated that television can add years to our lives (presumably so that we can watch more television and live even longer). Television has been blamed for increased promiscuousness, decreased literacy, increased drug usage, decreased family interaction, increased and decreased aggression, increased language homogenization, decreased movie attendance, increased prices at sporting events, decreased attention spans, and countless other increases and decreases. Two Montana psychologists have even reported findings that show that television causes young men to either (a) increase their desire to date attractive women or (b) decrease their desire to date unattractive women, depending on your point of view.

There is even some research (my own) that suggests that television can influence our evaluations of our own sex lives (not always for the better) and how we evaluate mentally retarded people.

Amid all these claims and scientific findings, the broadcasters' stance on television's effects remains the same: television does little more than entertain. If it has effects, they are at most minimal. Yet, the television people put a six-billion-dollar-a-year-bite on advertisers. We may think that a lot of the commercials that we see are stupid, but surely the advertisers aren't. But if the broadcasters are right and television has no effects, why do the advertisers pay six billion dollars annually to an industry that maintains that it has little impact other than entertainment?

Obviously, television has some impact. It may be true that statistics are like pet rocks, once you get them you can do what you want with them. Research statistics, however, have told us a good deal about television's influence. In fact, we now know conclusively and beyond a black and white or color shadow of a doubt that some programs under some conditions affect some people in some ways some of the time. profound

This scientifically and logically undeniable and nonrefutable solution to the "TV effects question," however, offers little solace and no guidance whatsoever to people like us who struggle with some really important questions like—Does television have effects? How does it affect us? How does it affect our children? Does it increase violence and aggression? When is it harmful? Helpful? Any one of us who owns a television, even if it serves little more apparent function than providing a convenient base and display area for our bowling trophies, has asked these and similar questions.

Why then don't we have good answers? One problem is the aforementioned pliability of statistics and the research that produces them. Broadcasters conduct and support research that shows effects beneficial to the maintenance of their very lucrative status quo. Educational and academic researchers perform studies that produce statistics that support their "elite" or "socially conscious" point of view. Surely, they claim and then demonstrate, Lucy and Ethel, Mork and Mindy, Cisco and Pancho, and Howard and Dandy can serve no useful purpose.

Another related problem in trying to understand television effects is that hardly anybody (least of all regular people) can understand the research and scholarly articles that supposedly prove and/or disprove those effects. The next time you read in the newpaper about that "noted television researcher" or that "respected social scientist" who has proven once and for all that there is a strong relationship between television viewing and reckless driving (I really read this), go read the original article, the one in which the expert presents his findings. Better yet, forget it. You will be confronted with a blizzard of F's, x^2's, and other strange notations.

Granted that we are offered a lot of confusing and oftentimes contradictory scientific evidence about how television may or may not influence us, but there is a larger problem. To borrow a phrase, we have met the problem and it is us. We all like television too much to really believe all the bad things that people are saying about it. Yet we are sensitive enough to our own lives and the lives of our children and friends not to be totally blind to television's effects. There develops, then, an uncomfortableness, a dissonance that must be resolved. One solution is to play it safe and stop watching. That, however, is too painful (which in itself should be evidence of television's influence). We're entertained by it. It is an inexpensive, enjoyable way to pass time. It provides us with much valuable information and entertainment. It serves as the basis for much of our conversation with our friends.

The other solution is much more palatable: ignore or discredit the evidence. That's easy, much of it is ignorable and discreditable. Anyway, there is enough contradictory scientific evidence and there are enough contradictory expert pronouncements that we can selectively ignore and discredit.

Another way that we deal with the television effects question is the "sure, but not me strategy." Nicholas Johnson, a former Federal Communication Commission commissioner, tells the story of a woman who remained unconvinced about television's impact on her buying judgments and habits. She was a mature, educated, responsible, independent person, she claimed, impervious to the mindless shilling of television advertisers. When asked what toothpaste she used, she responded that she used Gleem. Not because of the commercials, however, she said, but because she and her family couldn't brush after every meal. In case you've forgotten, Gleem, according to a series of ads they once ran, is the toothpaste for people who can't brush after every meal.

This denial strategy is oftentimes sincere. We are not really aware of television's influence on us and on those around us. Sometimes that influence is so subtle that we assume that that's "just the way we are." Sometimes that influence manifests itself or appears as part of some other set of influences, masking its connection to television.

Several years ago, for example, one of the major networks broadcast a film called *Fuzz*. An undistinguished movie, it is best remembered for two things. One is the scene in which Burt Reynolds dressed as a Catholic nun stumbled along, chasing a criminal on foot. Its other distinguishing feature was a scene in which a group of young toughs doused a drunk in gasoline and set him afire. This particular film would most likely have received all the attention of other television classics like "Me and the Chimp" or "My Mother the Car," except for the fact that within a week after it was aired, two similar murders-by-fire occurred, one in Boston, the other in Florida. After the Boston killing, the chief of police appeared on a local television news broadcast and offered his opinion as a professional law enforcement official. "See," he lectured the audience, "this is proof of the harmful effects of televised violence."

Inadvertently, he provided us with an argument against the existence of television effects. We don't burn winos. We don't even burn drug addicts. We would never do such a thing so, therefore, television violence must not affect us. But the fact that we did not and will probably never burn another person to death; the fact that we will never fly through the air in slow motion yelling ancient

Chinese epithets like "Kung Fu's" Kane; the fact that we will never climb to the top of our Spanish tiled house to pounce on the escaped convict who has kidnapped Peggy just as Mannix did every Sunday and then Wednesday night for eight years does not necessarily mean that we are free from television's influence. We *may* indeed be free of that influence. Or we may manifest that impact in other ways, verbal aggression, for example. We may not show the television-influenced aggression until our real world environment offers us enough incentive or reward to do so. We just don't know.

If we continue to look for dramatic evidence of television's influence (such as burning hoboes) before we accept the fact that that medium can influence us, we will always doubt television's potential influence. If we accept that television *can* influence us to some degree (even minimally), we can better understand how to avoid those effects that we consider harmful and maximize those we consider beneficial.

I admit that I am influenced by what I watch on television. Are you? Take a minute and answer (honestly) these ten questions:

1. Is the furniture in your den, living room, or wherever you keep the television situated around the television?

2. You are an employer who has two job candidates who are remarkably similar in every respect: experience, recommendations, appearance, hobbies, etc. Yet one reports that he favors Lowenbrau and Heineken beers and the other reports liking Budweiser and Schlitz. Would you, when forced to make a decision on whom to hire, choose the Heineken/Lowenbrau drinker?

3. Do you ever doubt that you are "woman enough" or "man enough" to satisfy your sexual partner?

4. Do you ever look at your mate and muse, "Why can't she/he be like Farrah, Hawkeye Pierce, or whoever?"

5. Do you find it difficult to sit through movies at the

theatre or through programs on the Public Broadcasting System, that is, programs without commercial breaks?

6. Do you believe that when Walter Cronkite says, "And that's the way it is, December 27, 1980," that that is the way it is?

7. Do you find that the amount of time that your family spends seated at meal time at home is growing shorter and shorter?

8. Do you ever find yourself intentionally understating the amount of television that you and your family watch?

9. Did you ever enter an important encounter (a job interview or first date, for example) and begin to worry about your breath, your deodorant, your dandruff, or your antiperspirant?

10. Do you ever find yourself saying or thinking, "Why can't I be like Mannix?" "Why can't I score like Hawkeye?" "Why aren't I indepedent like Mary Richards on the Mary Tyler Moore Show?"

If you've answered yes to some or most of these questions, you are under the influence of television! A yes answer to any of these suggests that you, and maybe your family, may be more susceptible than you realize. Remember, though, a yes answer to any of these ten questions is not necessarily a wrong or bad answer. It may be a bad answer for you and your family, it may be a good answer. Only you can decide. If you see your answers as negative, or if there are other television effects that you consider harmful to you or your family, you can do nothing about these negative effects unless you are aware that they exist. On the other hand, you will never be able to use television to its fullest as a beneficial medium unless you realize its potential for effects.

In December of 1978, Senator William Proxmire of Wisconsin gave his "Golden Fleece" award for waste in government spending to the Office of Education for its grant of $219,592 to Boston University. The Senator thought that their program to teach students how to become better television watchers was wasteful of tax-payers' money. Why don't colleges and universities teach people the "critical skills needed to watch football, shop for Christmas gifts, or shovel snow?" he asked. The answer is easy. Neither watching football, buying gifts, or shoveling snow influences what we buy, who we vote for, how we view ourselves and our fellow humans, how we perceive our government, how we dress for the weather, how we solve everyday problems, or how we spend dozens and dozens of hours every week. Our schools still teach reading, but our children spend more time watching the tube than they do with books. Our colleges still teach Shakespeare, Chaucer, and political science, yet our college students spend more time involved in television than they do in the fine arts and politics.

More aware, more "sophisticated" viewers can do two things. First, they can minimize harmful television effects and maximize beneficial ones. In the same way that an aware, sophisticated driver can avoid potentially dangerous driving hazards and make better use of available automotive aids, sophisticated viewers can control their television watching. Second, these "good viewers" can demand, through selective viewing or even non-viewing, programming that benefits their awareness and sophistication. Ultimately, this would make for better television which would result in better viewers who would, in turn, demand better television. The medium might then move from its vast wasteland, plug-in-drug, boob tube days to the fulfillment of its promise as a truly valuable mass medium.

Unaware, inactive, complacent, unsophisticated viewers perpetuate unaware, inactive, complacent, un-sophisticated, and unresponsive television. Aware, active, questioning, and sophisticated viewers present broad-casters with a challenge, one they implicitly admit that they need. As long as broadcasters continue to claim that

20

they give the viewers what they want, it behooves viewers who want good and useful television to want more.

In the chapters that follow, that's what we will try to do. We will look at what programs effect what people in what ways at what times. Hopefully, by relating our own viewing and our own experiences to the television effects issues that are discussed, we can come to better understand how our viewing affects us in what ways at what times. We may not rearrange our furniture, choose employees for reasons other than beer preference, become more satisfied with ourselves as lovers, see our mates as more attractive, or stop smelling our underarms in pressure situations. Or we may. Only we can decide what effects exist for each of us. More than anything, this is why there is no answer to the television effects question. The answer is different for all of us. But unless we have good solid information on which to base our answers for ourselves we will never come to a satisfactory conclusion.

CHAPTER 2

HOW CAN SOMETHING SO DUMB POSSIBLY HAVE ANY EFFECTS ON ME?

HOW TELEVISION EFFECTS HAPPEN

I consider television itself tantamount to a Milky Way bar; I call it mind candy. It feeds your need for sugar.

> —Brad Marks, television producer for the 1979 CBS "The National Collegiate Cheerleading Championships," quoted in an Associated Press story, April 16, 1979.

How Can Something So Dumb Have Any Effect?

If Mr. Marks is right that television is nothing more than mind candy, does that mean that we shouldn't worry about its effects? Eating too many Milky Ways will have an effect, why won't watching too much television have some impact?

If we were sitting in a bar or a lounge and an attractive member of the opposite sex took the seat next to one of us and said, "Hello, good looking, can I buy you a drink?" the first thing that we would probably do is try and figure out what he or she wanted. We might check this suitor out and make some initial judgment about looks, status, and most of all, intention.

"Hello, good looking, can I buy you a drink?" What does this mean? What can we expect? What happens if we say yes? What does this person want of me? Should we accept, decline, call the cops?

Or, we might encounter a different situation. Our little son returns from school and runs into our arms proclaiming his affection, "Mommy, Daddy, I love you!" "What's wrong?" most likely is our first reaction. Is it report card time? Did he break a window? What does he want now? All are quite logical questions we might (and probably do) ask.

Why do we question the words of a person who finds us attractive or a child who says he loves us? It's because we have learned to get along in our lives by making judgments about the communication that goes on around us. Very few of us would ever accept that offer of a drink without first doing some important reflection on its source and possible outcome. Very few of us ever accept interpersonal (that is everyday) communication at face value, even communication from people who are very close to us.

But almost all of us accept communication on television without question.

Think a minute about a favorite television program. Let's say it's "Laverne and Shirley," for example. What does this particular communication mean? What can we

24

expect if we accept its conventions, its portrayals of relationships, its solutions to problems? What does the producer want of us? What do the sponsors want? Should we accept the message as real or merely as fantasy? Even if we do take it as fantasy, what possible effect might it have?

You say that of course you know it's only a television program and no one could possibly think it's real. Take a moment and recount the plot of the most recent "Laverne and Shirley" or other program that you've seen. Do it out loud.

Did you hear yourself talking about Penny Marshall and Cindy Williams, or did you relate the doings of some people named Laverne, Shirley, Squiggy and Lenny? It's only conversational, you say, we call television characters by their media names because that's just the way we talk. But recount the plot of the film that you've seen most recently; you probably used the actors' and not the characters' names—Robert Redford, James Caan, Jane Fonda, and so on. Why? What's the difference between the media characters in our homes and the media characters at the theatre? It might be because we somehow see these television characters as real.

O.K. So you say so what, even if we do occasionally confuse the messages on the screen with real life it doesn't influence our behavior. But answer this question. There are no abstentions allowed, and your response again should be out loud. Out of what well known substance is the moon made? Cheese. You clearly and plainly said cheese. You know that the moon is made of rocks and dirt and the usual stuff, but your behavior showed something else, you said cheese. We may have the ability to discern fantasy from reality, but sometimes we are called upon to act without adequate time for reflection, as in this example, and the messages that have been delivered by television fantasies may influence our actions more than we think.

So you're still skeptical. You say, so O.K., I said

cheese. My confusion of fantasy and reality has no serious effect. So I said cheese, so what? Here's another question, then. I will name two individuals who have appeared often on television and then I'll ask you about them. Once again, your answer should be out loud and there are no abstentions allowed.

James Bond has often been played by Sean Connery. He is Agent 007, possessing the legal right to kill and he often does. He is tremendously handsome and has no trouble attracting beautiful women.

Russell Means is an American Indian. He is a leader in the American Indian Movement and a major participant in the Indian protests at Wounded Knee.

Those are the individuals. Here is the question: physically, that is, bodily, who smells better?

If you are honest, you will admit that you said James Bond. You probably never met either Mister Bond (or Connery) or Russell Means, and yet you answered the question in a certain way. Why do you suppose that Russell Means has a less pleasant smell than does James Bond? Somebody told you that American Indians smell bad. It wasn't your mother, it wasn't the checkout boy at the Stop and Shop.

More than likely it was television, and this is no harmless confusion of fact and fantasy. Not if you're an American Indian or any other group of people, or profession, or whatever that finds itself being dealt with, not as what they are, but as what people have come to see them as.

This is how television has effects: because we do not apply the same critical attention to it that we do other communications. We routinely accept its communication without question. It is a tremendous medium, it informs, entertains, teaches, enlightens. It does all this usually more pleasantly and easily than most face to face communication. But we risk taking the bad with the good if we are not as conscientious about our television communication as we are about our interpersonal communication.

So how do we become active, reflective, conscientious viewers? In truth, it isn't easy. We have all had a lifetime of real world communication and few of us would call ourselves masters of interpersonal communication. It can, however, be done.

The first thing that we need is some understanding of how that television communication may work to influence us.

Psychologist Albert Bandura has given widespread prominence to the idea of modeling. That is, television influences our behavior because we model or copy what we see on it. This modeling happens in two ways.

One way is imitation, copying of a specific behavior or set of behaviors. That means that we more or less duplicate what we see on the screen. We dress like Mary Tyler Moore. We greet our friends with Nanu Nanu. We bang our children over the head with a two by four board the way Moe hits Curley.

Stop, you say. None of us (I hope) does that. And that's the point. Although we can imitate what we see on television, very few of us do. Children often do, to the best of their ability, but adults know better. So while the potential for imitation from television exists, it really isn't of much help in our understanding of how television affects us.

The second way we model, however, is. It is called identification. It is much more difficult to see this modeling, yet it probably accounts for most of television's influence. It is a special kind of imitation that goes beyond specific behavior. It results from us wanting and trying to be like one or some television character. Sometimes it is a conscious attempt (remember Woody Allen in *Play it Again Sam* trying to identify with Bogart) and sometimes it's not. Instead of mimicking specific acts, we assume the general characteristics of the television character that those acts represent. For example, we may not imitate (copy) Mary Richard's specific dress and behavior, but we may identify with her general style of dress and way of living. We may never become associate producer of the local television news, but we want to become more independent, more professionally oriented, and so on.

We may never dress in loud clothes and suspenders and sit on our faces like Mork, but we may identify with his low-key, non-serious approach to dealing with the world.

And we will never hit our kids with two by fours, but we may come to see that general set of behaviors (striking or hitting) as a good and quick way to deal with someone who is annoying us. We may come to routinely use physical punishment to discipline our children.

The problem with identification is that we can't see it working. How can we tell that our desire to change jobs, our new carefree behavior with our friends, or our recent spanking of our children is the result of our identification with Mary, Mork, and Moe? We can examine our behaviors and try to trace their origins back to television, but this is difficult.

For one thing, where do parents, society, religious training, real world experiences, values, and beliefs enter into the picture? Because we cannot see the direct link between what's on the screen and our own behavior (as we sometimes can with imitation), it is hard to attribute effects to television, especially when there are so many other factors that may influence us.

Two mass communication researchers, Dr. Dennis Davis of the Cleveland State University and myself, have developed a way of looking at television effects that helps us understand how television influences our behavior while still accouting for the other possible influences, such as family and real world experience.

Basically, it assumes that we use all our experiences to deal with our environment. Some of those experiences come from our everyday lives and some come from television and other mass media. When we have to act in a given situation, we behave in a way that our experience tells us is more or less appropriate. This judgment, based on our experience, of how to act in a given situation is called a frame. Frames are social and/or personal definitions of situations that we use to organize our actions in those situations.

We build countless frames for the countless situations that we encounter every day.

The information that makes a frame for a given situation comes from all our experiences with that situation or situations like it. Often times those experiences come from the real world; often times they come from television portrayals; oftentimes they come from both.

In most instances it is almost impossible to determine where the information that we use to frame a specific situation came from. In the case of the Russell Means/James Bond example we can be fairly sure that it came from the mass media, probably television. Very few of us have even had real world experience with native American Indians, so our response was probably media influenced.

But what about less clear situations? What about our values, beliefs, self-concepts, and so on? How can we trace television's influence in these important parts of our lives? We have to become intelligent, reflective viewers. We need to question the messages that that medium delivers, the portrayal of the real world that it offers, our interpretation of these pictures, and the influence they may have on us.

In essence, we need to understand how television helps us frame different situations and what happens to us when we use those television-provided frames to deal with everyday life.

We already agreed that this is not easy, but the following eight chapters should help. Each offers some basics for beginning our reflection on the medium and its effects. We are worrying about money now more than ever and gasoline prices are limiting our leisure options, so we are staying at home more and spending more time in front of the screen. If we are to make the best use of this television time, now is when we should start asking the important questions about television's effects.

SUGGESTED ADDITIONAL READINGS

Davis, D. K. and Baran, S. J. *Mass Communication and Everyday Life: A Perspective on Theory and Effects.* Belmont, California: Wadsworth, 1981.

DeFleur, M. L. and Ball-Rokeach, S. *Theories of Mass Communication.* New York: David McKay, 1975.

Goffman, E. *Frame Analyis: An Essay on the Organization of Experience.* Cambridge, Mass.: Howard University Press, 1974.

Johnson, N. *How to Talk Back to Your Television Set.* New York: Bantam, 1970.

Johnson, N. *Test Pattern for Living.* New York: Bantam, 1972.

Klapper, J. *The Effects of Mass Communication.* New York: The Free Press, 1961.

Rivers, W. L. and Schramm, W. *Responsibility in Mass Communication.* New York: Harper and Row, 1969.

Shanks, B. *The Cool Fire: How to Make it in Television.* New York: Vintage Books, 1977.

Winn, M. *The Plug-in Drug.* New York: Viking, 1977.

CHAPTER 3

HOW CAN ANYTHING SO DUMB
HAVE ANY EFFECTS ON MY KIDS?

HOW TELEVISION EFFECTS
HAPPEN FOR KIDS

A high school freshman socializing after school with a girlfriend was shot and killed when the friend used a loaded gun while pretending to be actress Farrah Fawcett from the television series "Charlie's Angels."

—From an Associated Press news story, January 25, 1980

That killing received relatively little media attention. A young Florida boy, without ever really intending it, did much more to draw attention to television's effects on kids. He did more than the P.T.A., mass communications reasearchers, and all the other television violence critics combined. In 1977, while robbing the apartment of an elderly woman, he shot and killed her. The whole occurrence, he said, was just like what he had seen on "Kojak." The shooting and the subsequent trial were front page and prime time news material for some time.

Another unfortunate boy, this time a Los Angeles seven year old, was caught by his parents in the act of sprinkling ground glass into the family's lamb stew. He harbored no malice against his folks, he just wanted to see if it would work as well as it did when he saw it on television.

And just so we don't think that it's only little boys who do this sort of thing, a group of male *and* female Los Angeles pre-teens raped a nine year-old girl with the handle of a toilet plunger after seeing it done (with a soda bottle) on the NBC television movie, *Born Innocent.*

My kids would never do that, we say. Fair enough, they probably wouldn't. But what will and do they do as a result of their television watching? What do you think that they would have done in the following situation, one detailed in the 1978 report on advertising to children prepared by the Federal Trade Commission?

One Saturday morning Soupy Sales, a popular children's program host, asked his youthful viewers to go into Mommy's purse and Daddy's wallet and take out those dirty and wrinkled pieces of green paper and send them to old Soupy, in care of the address that he provided. Many of the children did. Would yours have relieved you of the burden of lugging around the dirty paper?

The FTC report was trying to make the point, one often forwarded by the people at Action for Children's Television, that our children are simply incapable of protecting themselves from television's impact. It isn't because they're stupid or dumb, or violent, or predisposed, it's because they are naive. They have very little real life experience against which to judge what they see on the screen. They have relatively few frames. Fantasy and reality are oftentimes difficult enough for adults to distinguish. But what about a small child?

At the 1972 U.S. Senate hearings on television effects, one mother, in talking about television commercials, put the problem this way when she asked one of the Senators, "Would you allow a salesman in your living room to sell something to a five year old?" When the Senator said no, he wouldn't, she asked, "Well, then, why do you let him sell to five year olds on television?" Why do we assume that our kids are free from television's influence? We would not let a salesperson pitch his or her wares to our kids, or would we? Almost all of us let television salespeople sell to our children every day. We even encourage our youngsters to go and sit in front of the screen, making it easier for the advertisers to reach them.

We do not expect our children to read books and newspapers, they're too young to understand, we say. Yet we put them in front of the television set (every bit as much an adult medium as books and newspapers) and expect that they will react and be influenced no differently than we.

And do we put them in front of the set! Average American children aged three, four, and five watch nearly 55 hours of television a week. This is over 60% of the time that they are awake. High school kids in the U. S. attend school for 980 hours a year, but they watch television, on the average, for 1340 hours. Each year, all the kids in America watch more than 90 billion hours of television. That's a lot of television. All of this viewing must have some influence, but what and how?

It's much easier to talk about effects for kids than it is for adults. We seem to be more willing to accept that television can have influence if it's on someone else. But more than that, it's easier to understand how someone as fresh and naive as a child can be influenced. This should give some support to the notion of framing that we talked about in the last chapter. The reason kids seem more influencable is because they have less experience—less information to use in framing different situations. The little boy wearing Daddy's hat and the little girl putting on Mommy's make-up are really attempting to frame different situations (going to work, going on a date) using information provided by Mom and Dad. They have no experience with work and social life, so they frame these situations in the way that someone they trust—their parents—would. But the truth is, parents are playing less and less a role in providing that important socializing information. Television may be taking it over.

A well-known sociologist, Urie Bronfenbrenner, wrote that our playgrounds are getting bigger and our backyards are getting smaller. He was telling us that our children are growing up increasingly outside the family influence.

More and more mothers are going to work. Both mothers and fathers alike have more outside-the-home interests than ever before, and with the rate of divorce as high as it is, the U. S. Census Bureau predicts that forty-five percent of the children born in these times will live at least part of their childhood in a one-parent family. All these factors reduce the amount of time and contact that parents have with their kids. Even the very best parents find it difficult to give their children the attention that they themselves received from their own folks.

Not only are we spending less and less time with our kids, leaving them free to be with friends and television, but a lot of us are content to use television as a baby sitter. We plop our kids down and tell them to watch while we're busy doing other things.

So there are our children, naive, inexperienced. They want and need information about how to deal with their world, and a large amount of that information comes from television; but because of the way they develop intellectually, they cannot discriminate between what is real or fantasy and what is useful and useless on television.

From the time a child is born, he or she begins to learn from the environment. Most of the early learning comes about through chance interactions with things in the world. This is why really young children come to see the world as self-centered. Its existence is defined by the contact the child has had with it, it exists only inasmuch as it affects and is influenced by the child. All parents have seen their children hide their eyes from something that scares them. If they cannot see it, children reason, it does not exist. But as they get older, they come to learn that there is a world apart from themselves that must be dealt with and understood. Where do they get that information?

Until the time that they are about two years old, parents are children's primary source of information about the world around them. They define children's worlds for them and they give meaning to its occurrences and situations. After that stage, however, things begin to change. Children enter what developmental and child psychologists call the operational stage. This period in the child's psychological growth and social development continues until around twelve years old.

In this period of maturation children tend to accept experiences in their world at face value. They have not yet developed the mental ability to evaluate and test new experiences and information against existing experiences and information. In other words, they are unable to question the usefulness of the information they learn.

At the next stage of psychological development, cognitive thought, they begin to see new experiences and information as propositions to be tested and evaluated. They begin to learn that experiences can be framed in different ways. But until that time, children are at the mercy of the environment. They define situations as the situation

35

demands. This is exactly why the Action for Children's Television people argue that all television commercials aimed at kids under twelve years old are inherently deceptive—kids are in a stage of psychological and cognitive development that renders them incapable of judging the intent or merits of the message. Kids in the operational stage accept information naively.

That's why young children appear so susceptible to television's impact: for them it has the weight of reality. Next time that you are in the supermarket, take two different brands of cereal, one a name brand—Cap'n Crunch or Fruit Loops or something—and a store brand. Ask your child which he or she prefers. You know right now that the choice will be the name brand cereal.

Children are not born with an innate preference for name brand products, nor do we rock them on our knees saying, "Remember, baby, always buy name brands because they insure quality."

Somewhere along the line in your child's growth he or she learned to prefer certain cereals—that is, heavily advertised cereals. Why? Because he or she had no way to evaluate the information being provided by the television. When in the supermarket and faced with the situation of having to make a choice, your child frames it in the way that the television commercial instructed.

Ask your child (if he or she is old enough) to spell relief. You have already said to yourself, "R-O-L-A-I-D-S," but that's material for a later chapter. A third grade teacher asked her class to spell relief and over half of her students spelled it R-O-L-A-I-D-S. With only a small amount of spelling skill of their own these children accepted the information offered by the tube, the commercial's spelling became the reality.

As children get older, though, their mental abilities grow. They become better able to judge new information and experiences. They become better equipped to evaluate television messages. This is called adult discount. This

36

means that the potential influence of children's use of television messages is reduced—or discounted—because they are more able to compare the information to the real world. It's like seeing your parents putting toys under the Christmas tree. No longer do the stories about Santa have any impact, because your real world experience gives you a basis against which to judge those stories.

How powerful is the adult discount? It depends on the child and his or her interaction with television and the family. For the fifteen year old Minnesota boy who jumped to his death from a bridge in August of 1979 because "Battlestar Galactica" was cancelled it was probably not very strong. But you can help your children develop their own adult discount, even when they are quite young.

The way that this is done goes by several names. Sometimes it's called intervention, sometimes interpretation, sometimes receivership skills. But whatever the label, it involves interacting with your children to help them become more aware viewers. You can help them improve what is called their visual literacy. We all spend time working with our children to improve their reading and writing literacy. We can do the same for their visual literacy if we want to.

The scientific literature demonstrates that this works for a number of reasons. For one, the fact that you watch with your children and talk with them about the program increases the amount of contact that you share. Because you comment on the program, children can come to understand that your allowing them to watch so much television does not mean implied approval of what is on the screen.

But most important, the information that you provide and the instruction that you offer can help your children better understand and utilize what is on the screen.

Intervention works something like this. Sit and watch a program with your children (we'll choose a long time favorite, "The Three Stooges"). You cannot change what is on the screen. You cannot prohibit them from watching—it will only increase the show's attractiveness and the kids at school will think they're creeps because they don't watch television. What you can do is use that material for your children's own good.

Here's what's on the screen: Moe hits Curley over the head with a board; Curley wipes his head, says "woop woop woop," and takes a swing at Moe; it misses and strikes Larry on the side of the face and knocks him into a barrel of water; he gets out, gets a shotgun and shoots Curley in the bottom; Curley rushes to the barrel and dips his tail in the water and steam rises.

We'll talk more about it in a later chapter, but this is probably the worst kind of television violence that there is. The kids see (and possibly learn) the aggressive behaviors. They see none of the harmful consequences of violence. They see violence presented as an acceptable means of dealing with other people. And they see it, not as serious and dangerous activity, but as fun and funny. What's a parent to do?

What we do is intervene between the set and the child. We help our children interpret these goings on so that the information they provide can be used to frame situations that our kids will encounter in their everyday lives. We might handle it this way: "Now Junior and Missey, why did Moe hit Curley with that board? That's right, because he put tacks in the wedding cake and everyone's teeth broke. Is that a good reason for hitting him with a stick? Why didn't he tell the people not to eat the cake and then talk to Curley about being less careless?"

Give the children time to answer. Talk with them as well as to them.

"What do you really think happens when someone gets hit with a stick or shot with a gun? It hurts real bad, you're right. Sticks should never be used to hit people, they can make them bleed or blind them. And guns, you know that they are not toys, that they can kill someone."

Again, talk with those children. If the intervention becomes a lecture or an unwanted interruption of the program it will fail. If it is an enjoyable, friendly chat between parent and child it can do wonders for the family and for speeding up our children's adult discount.

This is not to say that intervention is a snap. It takes a lot of skill on the part of the parent. As we all know, the line between lecture and conversation is a fine one when dealing with our children. There is also the problem of time. Few of us have the time to watch a lot of television with our children. If done well, however, the viewing skills that are passed on to children in our intervention will be carried over into their watching even when we're not around.

Another problem is that not all of our children's viewing is as easily interpreted as the Three Stooges beating up on one another. How do we easily explain that not everyone has a double martini when they return home from work? How do we easily explain that the taking of two aspirin will not immediately reduce family tensions? Television violence is relatively easy to interpret for our children because aggression and violence are often real factors in their lives. Alcohol and pills, on the other hand, may be a little too far removed from them. What may be happening, then, is that children are learning various values surrounding these things even before they are able to actually deal with them. Here is where we have to hope that the receivership skills that we help our children develop can carry over to many types of programming and television information.

There is a final, more philosophical question that is associated with intervention.

Why do we have to intervene at all? Why does a medium that is licensed to serve us create work for us? Because in our country we have opted for a commercial system of television broadcasting and, in truth, the overwhelming majority of us are satisfied with the television that we receive. Few of us would recommend or accept censorship. Given this, we can do very little to alter the medium. We can do very little to alter or speed up the intellectual development of our children. What we can influence is the communication between the two, we can change what the child learns from the set. Intervention is not easy, but in the absence of any dramatic change in our contemporary system of broadcasting, it is one of the best alternatives for helping our children deal with television.

SUGGESTED ADDITIONAL READING

Melody, W. *Children's TV: The Economics of Exploitation.* New Haven: Yale University Press, 1973.

Noble, G. *Children in Front of the Small Screen.* Beverly Hills: Sage, 1975.

Schramm, W., Lyle, J., and Parker, E. *Television in the Lives of Our Children.* Stanford: Stanford University Press, 1961.

CHAPTER 4

HOW COME
FARRAH AND FONZIE
NEVER GET ZITS?
TELEVISION
AND SELF-EVALUATION

Out in the unreal reaches of sponsor land, something horrible happens along about the 30th birthday. People under 30 have supple bodies and glistening hair. People over 30 have throbbing headaches and distress in the lower tract. The good life ends when maturity begins. Constipation begins at 40.

> —"A Grim TV Tale," by John Ed Pearce, *The Cleveland Plain Dealer Sunday Magazine,* September 17, 1972.

Now comes the heavy stuff, you and television. Up until now you've probably accepted that your kids can and may be influenced by what's on the tube. But what about you? Even the most skeptical television viewers have to admit that their choice of car, style of dress, and selection of brands is somehow influenced by television. But what about the important things, what about how television influences how we see ourselves?

Remember the Woody Allen movie, *Play It Again Sam*? If you did, I'll remind you of the plot and if you didn't, here's how it went. Woody Allen was a perpetually frustrated bachelor because he could not attract, seduce, and treat women the way that Humphrey Bogart did. So obsessed was he with living up to Bogey's standards, that the spirit of Humphrey Bogart would follow him around and Allen would ask the ghost what he should do next with the woman, how he was doing so far, and so on.

Only in the end, when he gave up a married woman to her rightful husband (like Bogey did in *Casablanca*) could Allen hold his head high. The character that Woody Allen played was so tied up with the image of Humphrey Bogart that he judged himself and his worth by the standards established by that ideal.

That's not such a bad thing, you might say. We need more heroes. We need impressive characters that we can emulate. This is true, but only to a certain point. The unfortunate fact is that there are very few heroes after whom we can pattern our lives. There are, however, countless and ever present stereotypes that come to be seen, not as heroes, but as representatives of the norm. These images are easy to accept because they are usually attractive, and they are always present. Most of us, however, cannot meet the standards that they establish and how we deal with this "failure" has a lot to do with how we judge ourselves.

Take breasts, for example. What makes a good breast? Biologically, a good breast is one that can meet the feeding requirements of the mother's offspring. But there is also a cultural or social definition of what constitutes good breasts. In the 1940's the Rita Hayworth look was in but by the 1960's flat chests were seen as healthy and attractive—remember Twiggy? Now with the 80's underway, full, robust breasts are again considered attractive.

Many men may think that they always liked big breasts or they say that breast size never really mattered, but how many women have you known who are otherwise intelligent and secure but who worry themselves silly about their chests. "I'm too small." "I'm too big." "I'm too firm." "I'm too soft." "I don't have enough definition." "God, I need something that will lift and separate." These are all worries that we often hear women express. They're sort of funny until we think about those women who allow their concern about their breasts—concern that is created because they evaluate themselves against some external standard—to influence their self-concept.

In an intriguing book, *Breasts: Women Speak About Their Breasts and Their Lives* (Summit Books), artists Daphna Ayalah and Isaac Weinstock examine the "perfect breast" phenomenon. They wrote that the media's use of breasts to sell cars, magazines, detergent, and toothpaste has created an image of the "ideal breast." That image, though, is far from the reality of actual breasts. The ones that we see on the television are usually propped up or accentuated with make-up. In addition, actresses who play female characters are chosen in large part because of their large parts (remember Loni Anderson on "WKRP in Cincinnati"?) and male characters usually comment on or admire big breasts (remember all the guys on "WKRP in Cincinnati"?), so we see a television world where most women have "perfect breasts" and most men find them attractive because of it. Ayalah and Weinstock wrote that this presentation inevitably leads to one thing, women will almost always find something to criticize about their own breasts.

We all know men like the character in *Play It Again*

Sam and women who are self-conscious about their breasts. How do people allow their evaluations of themselves to become so integrally tied to norms or images provided by the mass media?

We don't do it on purpose. Few of us will turn on television with the thought in mind, "I think I'll watch M*A*S*H* and get some pointers from Hawkeye on how to handle women," or "I think I'll watch Charlie's Angels and get an idea of how to wear my breasts this week." We watch television to be entertained. But engaging in that form of mass communication has the same effect as engaging in communication with the rest of our environment, it provides us with information that we can use to frame things in the real world. Social science tells us that an important result of communication is that it helps us frame ourselves, it helps create our self-concept. There is no reason to separate mass communication from everyday communication.

Our self-concept is the picture we develop of ourselves; exactly who and what we are. It influences not only our perception of our self-worth, but it affects how we act in different situations because we behave based on our picture of ourselves. Our self-concept develops and becomes established based on our communication with the environment. In effect, we become what the world says we are, or even more precisely, what we let the world tell us we are. Our self-concept is not based on what others think of us, but on what we think they think of us. A woman may have no personal dissatisfaction with her breasts, for example, but if communication with her environment keeps telling her that others think that she has bad breasts (for whatever reason), that information could alter her self-concept.

Skeptical? In 1978, two Montana psychologists discovered some interesting evidence to support the idea that television's beauties do influence our evaluation of real life women, and by extension, their evaluations of themselves.

Douglas Kendrick and Sara Gutierres devised an experiment in which they had a male college student enter a dormitory room where a dozen or so other college men had just finished watching "Charlie's Angels." He showed them a picture of a woman who was supposedly coming to town that weekend and who needed a date. No way, was the response, there were no takers. The guys who had just finished watching the three Angels didn't think that the woman in the photograph was good looking enough to warrant a date.

The same student then took the same photograph to a room where the guys were not watching television. Those men rated the woman in the photograph as much more attractive and desirable as a date. There were even takers for the blind date offer. The girl in that picture, regardless of her actual looks, just could not measure up against Farrah and the other Angels. For some reason, however, when she did not have to compete with Charlie's threesome she did O.K.

The same researchers showed some other men a series of ads that featured beautiful women. They showed another group of men photos of regular, non-media women. When they asked all of them to evaluate the attractiveness of a woman in another picture, those gents who had seen the advertising models rated her as unattractive, while those who had seen "real" women found her to be pretty good-looking.

What does this do to a woman's self-evaluation? If television sets standards of beauty that are unattainable for most women, and men evaluate women on that basis, female self-concept is bound to suffer. Women may come to judge themselves against a standard that they cannot achieve.

And what about men? Dan Tana, Hawkeye Pierce, Jim Rockford. All tall, good looking, strong, smart, tender, witty, or, in other words, perfect men. How many men in the real world can measure up to the standard or norm created by these imposing characters?

There is a theory that explains this phenomenon, it is called cultural norms theory. Cultural norms theory says that because of repeated presentations of something in the mass media (attractive men and women, in this case), it comes to be seen as the norm; that is, it comes to be seen as what actually is. We are shown tall, leggy, big busted, beautiful women and tall, handsome, strong but sensitive men in almost all television programming, so we come to see those images as the norm, and if we don't measure up to that image, we are not normal.

Still skeptical? Try this little experiment. Get a pen and draw the outline of a dime in the appropriate size without looking at one before you draw.

Now get a real dime and put it over your artwork. The actual dime is bigger than the one you drew. Inflation is bad and money, especially coins, is worth very little. Our unconscious evaluation of a ten-cent piece forces us to demean its worth, so much so that we represent it as even smaller than it really is. Our perception of that coin influenced how we represented it.

Is it inconceivable, then, that our perceptions and evaluations of ourselves—something that is reinforced every time we switch on the television set—can influence how we represent ourselves?

SUGGESTED ADDITIONAL READINGS

Casty, A. *Mass Media and Mass Man.* New York: Holt, Rinehart and Winston, 1973.

Rosen, M. "Farrah Fawcett-Majors Makes Me Want to Scream!" *Redbook Magazine,* September, 1977, 102-109.

Skornia, H. J. *Television and Society.* New York: McGraw-Hill, 1965.

Stein, B. *The View from Sunset Boulevard: America as Brought to You by the People Who Make Television.* New York: Basic Books, 1979.

CHAPTER 5

ISN'T THE EARTH SUPPOSED TO MOVE?

TELEVISION AND OUR SEXUAL SELVES

Scenes of crashing waves or bursts of fireworks used to symbolize it in the movies. But many of us who are now adults remember our first fumbling attempt at intercourse as something of a fizzle. Either we came to it with such guilt feelings . . . or with such unrealistic expectations that it was hardly possible to relax and enjoy it.

—"Right Now," *McCall's,* October, 1973.

Get a Triumph and get a piece . . . of history. Does she or doesn't she? The toothpaste with sex appeal. This tube changed my love life. I'm Carol, fly me. My men wear English Leather or they wear nothing at all. You're not getting older, you're getting better. Take it off . . . take it all off. I like it long. I'd like to flick his Bic. With Old Spice the invitation is clear.

If these everyday television slogans ring no bells, maybe these everyday plots from television commercials will:

—The little pipsqueak of a man following the rugged sailor around Bangkok, watching him from hiding as this good-looking stud who used Old Spice picks up dozens of women.

—The woman who passes an old boyfriend from school in a hotel lobby and is crushed because he does not recognize her. She buys the bra that lifts and separates and, the next time they pass, he immediately notices her. (Two important questions can be raised here. One, why is this woman hanging around hotel lobbies looking for men? Two, why does the guy recognize her only after she changes the look of her breasts? Didn't he ever look at her face?)

—Two guys (girls) in their early twenties talking on their boat (in their ski lodge). One has just spent $50 for a new sweater (skirt) in hopes that it will attract the attention of a good-looking woman (man) that he (she) is taken with. The friend solves the problem by suggesting that the guy (girl) put his (her) money where his (her) mouth is. The ensuing purchase of Ultra-Brite wins the guy (girl) the affection of the longed-for girl (guy) and changes his (her) love life.

If none of these standard plots is familiar, maybe you are familiar with some of these programs. They all depend primarily on what television people call T and A (for Tits and Ass) or jiggle programs:

50

"WKRP in Cincinnati"
"Charlie's Angels"
"Three's Company"
"Flying High"
"Love Boat"
"Fantasy Island"
"American Girls"
"Soap"
"Super Train"
"Network Battle of the Super Stars"
"Battle of the NFL Cheerleaders"

And, of course, for serious sex, there are the soap operas, "Dallas," and the detective shows that deal at various times with female prostitution, male prostitution, child prostitution, white slavery, rape, woman beating, and homosexuality.

Unless you haven't been watching, there's a lot more sex on television today than in the days when couples were shown sleeping in twin beds and when Lucy could not use the word "pregnant" on the "I Love Lucy" show, even though she was actually and clearly pregnant—the program censors finally allowed "in a family way." And a lot of people are upset about the "sex on television" problem. Complaints about sex on television to the Federal Communication Commission have increased to record numbers in the last several years. Personally, I don't like sex on television—I fell off once and hurt my back (bad joke, sorry).

The PTA, various church-affiliated organizations, and many other citizen's groups have begun organized efforts against the influx of sexually oriented material on television. Their efforts, however, while well intentioned, not only are doomed to failure, but they just don't make sense. Like the residents of Clarkstown, N. Y. who apparently wanted no person to play censor for them (they appointed a blind man in 1973 to head their obscenity committee to judge the value of movies, bar acts, and

51

magazines), few of us are willing to let the PTA, church groups, or citizen's organizations tell us right from smut.

Another reason (besides our obvious and traditional distaste for censorship) is that few of us can believe that the simple and non-graphic portrayals of sex and male/female behavior that do appear on television can possibly influence us. And it's true, few of us get sexually excited or sexually aroused while watching "Three's Company" or other television programs.

There is, however, a different kind of effect that may be possible, one that is less obvious but more likely. It has to do with the television portrayals of men and women dealing with one another and how they influence the way we frame our own encounters with the opposite sex. It may be that these simple portrayals help us develop a certain set of expectations about sex that cannot be met. Or, in the language of the last chapter, they help create a norm that may be unreal or unattainable.

Put yourself in this situation. You wonder why your partner loses interest. It seems that you hear, "Not tonight," "Not now," and "Not here," with depressing and increasing regularity. More frightening, you hear yourself offering those same put-offs. To borrow a line from an old commercial, you seem to be doing it more, but enjoying it less.

Remember the movie *Annie Hall*. The heroine needed to get high on pot to find pleasure and excitement in love making. When forced to have sex "straight," she mentally stepped out of herself and began sketching and doodling to pass the time until her impassioned lover was satisfied. What Annie faced, and what increasing numbers of real people may be facing, is dissatisfaction or boredom with sex. Making it may not be making it for a lot of folks.

The problem may be an old one with a new wrinkle: competition from a more exciting and glamorous source. But the twist is that the competitor is not the traditional "other woman" or "other man," instead it may well be television. Television's electronic bed-wreckers are no mere wretches or gigoloes. They are always there, able to change their looks, personality, and guile in a wink, and they are particularly insidious, because they are above suspicion.

There is some current scientific evidence that suggests that television portrayals of male/female relationships may well be hurting your love life. Nobody's sexual socialization or sexual awareness develops through an orderly process of appropriate information intake that leads to sexual maturity and competence. Instead, we hear conflicting, half-baked, semi-uninformed, guilt-laden, and ego-bound explanations and descriptions of sex that leave us wondering how the birds and bees ever learned to do those things that have made them famous.

Making matters even worse, the only examples that we seem to have when we are growing up are those same birds and bees (and occasionally, a dog or two). American cultural norms of privacy do not allow us the direct viewing of sexual exchange, so we come to face one of the most important facets of adult life without the benefit of live models after whom we might pattern ourselves. What is left to the maturing person is information from friends, school, parents, church, and the mass media, particularly television. This guidance is, at best, lousy. At its worst, it may be damaging to our successful sexual maturation.

We might logically think that because there is no "real" sex on television (as opposed to in the movies) that it can't possibly influence us. But that's the point. The movies may show us a lot more actual sexual activity than does television, but it also shows us somewhat more realistic sex—the problem as well as the pleasures, the failures as well as the successes, the casual sex as well as the meaningful relationships.

Television, with its implied sex occurring off screen or during commercials, with its ads that tell us that successful

53

and pleasant sex is only a toothpaste away, and with its leering, double entendre-laden T and A shows, help us frame sex as something that is easily available, easily engaged in and trouble free, quite casual, and tremendously important to the development of a good self-concept. You are a loser until you buy this cologne and get yourself a sex mate.

This potential damage is reflected in the big question that every one of us has asked ourselves at least once on the long trail to adulthood, "Am I normal?" We worried about the size and looks of our sex organs and about our attractiveness to the opposite sex. We worried whether we would ever get to have a sexual partner at all and, if we ever did, would we be good in bed. It may well be that many of us worried that we were homosexual. Then, it happened! We found someone who did not mind our too big or too small breasts, our too big or too small thighs, our use of the wrong shampoo . . . and then . . . then . . . No fireworks, no waves dashing furiously against the rocky shore, no earth moving beneath us as we trembled in orgasmic delight.

What may have happened, and what may still be happening, is that the fact cannot live up to the fiction. Frustration and dissatisfaction with our and our partner's sexual performance is a normal reaction, given the pictures we have developed in our minds, or in other words, how we have come to frame sex. For many people, television portrayals of sexual behavior raise expectations of sexual pleasure to such a level that frustration and dissatisfaction are the only logical reactions when we actually have a chance to test ourselves against those television images. On television there is no failure, no fumbling, no blood, no pain, no guilt. Couples easily move into and out of all types of encounters, casual and meaningful. In fact, because television cannot deal with sex in a realistic way, we are presented with images of male/female encounters that are totally unreal and, therefore, unattainable.

We see the back of Charlie's well-groomed head, as several Hefneresque beauties stroke his legs and back. He has "business" to attend to, he chortles into the phone. At the other end, the Angels and Bosley squeal with delight. The screen goes dark. Commercial . . . Hawkeye enters the nurses' quarters and announces that he is "off-duty" and available and that the supply tent is equally available. The line of takers forms, he smiles, the screen does dark. Commercial.

At home, "business" usually refers to bills, cleaning, making the bed, and raking the yard. "Off-duty" usually means watering the plants, bills, cleaning, making the bed, and raking the yard. Stated simply, our satisfaction or dissatisfaction with ourselves and our partners as sexual beings may well rest in part on how we view television sex. People who see television portrayals of male/female relationships as real (more than half in two recent studies that I conducted) are more likely to be unhappy or dissatisfied with their own love making and sex lives. These television sex believers also see themselves as inferior lovers. Apparently, these viewers are unable to meet the expectations that they have developed through watching television.

There is some good news, though. Age and experience seem to help. As we get older and begin to learn about sex first hand, television's influence over sexual satisfaction begins to decline. The old saying must be true, nothing succeeds like success. As we add to our psychological storehouse of sexual experience, not only do we become more proficient and satisfied, but we also learn the truth about the accuracy of television portrayals of sex, we come to frame sex better. What of those people, however, who never recover from those initial and often inevitable disappointments? What about those people, and we all know at least one, who still and always will live in a land of television make-believe?

Can television really have that kind of influence over our sex lives? How happy were you with your performance on your first time in bed with a man or woman? How did that first love making experience influence how you felt about future sexual encounters? Have you ever wished that love making was as exciting as some mental standard that you've developed? Where did those standards or images of "exciting sex" come from?

Ask your partners these same questions. They may have already given you their answer. How long have they been suffering from those night-time headaches?

SUGGESTED ADDITIONAL READINGS

Baran, S. J. "How TV and Film Portrayals Affect Sexual Satisfaction in College Students." *Journalism Quarterly,* 53, 1976, 468-473.

Baran, S. J. "Sex on TV and Adolescent Sexual Self-Image." *Journal of Broadcasting,* 20, 1976, 61-68.

Morse, H. L. "The Influence of Mass Media on the Sex Problems of Teenagers." *Journal of Sex Research,* 2, 1966, 27-35.

Scott, J. E. and Franklin, J. L. "Sex References in the Mass Media." *Journal of Sex Research,* 9, 1973, 196-209.

CHAPTER 6

JUST WHAT
DOES OZZIE NELSON DO
FOR A LIVING?

TELEVISION AND MARRIAGE
AND THE FAMILY

I'd found my prince, and I knew I was supposed to be
thrilled. We got engaged, and I thought I would sud-
denly be swept away, cared for, nurtured. I got to
hate my fiance when I realized he wasn't going to fly
me to the moon. There he was, expecting as much
from me as I was expecting from him.

> —"Marriage Jitters," *Glamour*, May,
> 1979.

Just What Does Ozzie Nelson Do for a Living?

Remember "The Adventures of Ozzie and Harriet," the television program about the Nelson family and their two sons, David and Ricky? One of the questions that was asked about that show for its fourteen year run on ABC and in the years since that it has been in re-runs is what did Ozzie do for a living? He was always home. The boys would come home from school in the afternoon, Ozzie would be there. Harriet would come home from grocery shopping in the morning, Ozzie would be waiting for her. Thorny Thornberry, the neighbor, would visit the Nelsons in the evening, there was old Oz.

He didn't seem to have a job, and work or the office were never mentioned. His family, however, lived in a beautiful home, the boys had musical instruments, not to mention sound-proof bedrooms in which to practice, they had a car, and Ozzie had what appeared to be a lifetime supply of cardigan sweaters.

When once asked by Johnny Carson about where all this wealth came from even though he apparently held no job, Ozzie responded that he was supposed to have been a brain surgeon. That may be true, but there was nothing in the program itself to prove it.

Not that Ozzie was alone in holding mysterious employment. For six years Ward Cleaver (Beaver's father) went daily to "the office." What kind of office it was was never mentioned. The same sort of thing was happening on "The Donna Reed Show" and "Father Knows Best." Dr. Alex Stone (Donna's husband, played by Carl Betz) was a pediatrician and was often being called on to administer to his patients, but we never saw him at work and his profession never infringed on the tranquillity of his and Donna's household. The father who knew best, Jim Anderson (played by Robert Young) was an insurance salesman, but we knew that because we were told, not because his work was a part of the program.

When characters held blue collar jobs, on the other hand, their work did tend to be more a part of the program (Chester A. Riley, the airplane factory worker in "The Life of Riley" and Ralph Kramden, the bus driver in "The Honeymooners," for example), but they were usually depicted as kind-hearted but bumbling fools. Their jobs were never shown, they were only used to provide joke material.

For years, television families were presented in just this way—unrealistically. If the father did work, it was either at some seemingly trouble-free, high-paying job or he was a slob who had to labor for a living, although we never saw him work. Mothers never held jobs. The parents were always available when the kids needed them and there was no problem that Mom and Dad could not solve. Money was never a problem, in fact, it was never mentioned. Almost everyone owned a home and car, had nice clothes, and ate full-balanced meals every night.

The same goes for television marriages, they were just as unrealistic. The wife never worked, both partners were supportive, and if trouble ever did arise, it was surely solvable before the last commercial. There were no problems with paying bills, infidelity, sexual incompatibility, disagreements about childbearing and childrearing. Marriage was as easy as falling off a log. Maybe the Kramdens had trouble, and even though they were clumsy laborer types, they still worked them out in thirty minutes.

Television families and marriages, fortunately, have become a little more realistic. No longer are all families financially well-heeled or blue collar because they're stupid—Archie Bunker worked on a loading dock and struggled to buy his neighborhood bar, and the Evanses on "Good Times" were a proud but poor welfare family. We even see families and couples dealing with realistic problems like drugs, bills, drinking, the maturation of their children, gambling, independence of the wife, and so on.

But there is still that one very important piece of unreality—all problems are solved before the last commercial. Some programs, "All in the Family" is a good example, try to get around that problem by continuing stories over a couple of weeks, but the medium of television demands that problems be resolved in some finite period of time, usually defined in terms of half-hours—one episode, two episodes, and so on. Marriage may no longer be as easy as falling off a log, but we are given the definite impression that when problems do arise, they are pretty much solvable and all will be well in the end.

Soap opera fans are probably getting annoyed, feeling that their programs are not guilty of this problem. It is true, soaps do not solve their marital and family problems in neat half-hours. Their nonrealism comes from the length of time it takes for problems and solutions to develop—two-year pregnancies, for example—and the fact that the soap opera citizens' problems are not real problems—unless we are on our third husband or wife, paying for our eighth abortion, and just returning to heterosexual activity after experimenting with homosexuality that resulted from our father's disclosure that he is a defrocked priest.

What happens, then, if we come to judge our own marriages and families according to this information that we get from television? What happens when we frame our own real world experiences in terms of the television marriages and families that we view night after night and afternoon after afternoon?

These are particularly important concerns given the poor state of matrimony in this country. In 1940 there were only two divorces for every thousand people, but by 1978 that number was up to 5.1 divorces per thousand people. In 1978 there were 2.2 million marriages and 1.1 million divorces. The U.S. Census Bureau has predicted that if the current rate of divorce continues, 40 percent of the marriages that will happen in the next several years will end in divorce. As it stands now, 45 percent of the kids alive today will spend at least part of their childhood in a one-parent household.

There are a number of reasons for this increase in failed marriages; differing values among husbands and wives, getting married at too early an age, premarital and early marital pregnancy, and so on. There is one reason, however, that is particularly important to our discussion: people who get married today are not very well prepared for that adventure; we have very little reliable information about marriage available to us. There are no schools for marriage; there is really no place to learn about the trials, tribulations, and rigors of matrimony before we enter that ostensibly life-long state. And Ozzie, Harriet, and Jim Anderson notwithstanding, marriage is rarely as easy as falling off a log.

The *Glamour* magazine from which this chapter's opening quote was taken related the story of "Ann." Her situation might help us better understand what the consequences of this lack of valuable information might be. It seems that Ann had found her prince. He was going to sweep her away, the earth would move, and the waves would crash against the shores. Being married to this man was to be heaven. She came to hate him, however, when she discovered that he would not be able to fly her to the moon. She was expecting things from him (and marriage) that could not be delivered. Where did these expectations come from? In other words, how did poor Ann come to see marriage in such a way that she ended up being disappointed? There is a growing amount of scientific evidence that television might have been one source of inaccurate information.

There is a wealth of research work that demonstrates that television presents very stereotyped and inaccurate portrayals of marriage and marriage roles. Almost all contemporary male television characters, for example, are employed, while only about forty percent of the female characters seem to have work other than the household variety. Wives are usually presented as subservient to and dependent on their husbands, having little initiative of their own. Women in commercials are depicted as dimwitted and interested only in matters such as water spots on the glassware and rings around the collar. Men judge their wives' worth on their ability to keep water spots off the glassware and rings away from their collars.

Couple these representations of husbands and wives with television's habit of showing loving, happy families easily solving their problems, and it becomes easy to see that the tube may be a bad place to get marriage information.

Where else can we get that information? Our parents are usually not very good sources. We are too close to them, it is too easy to justify their behavior in their marriage as idiosyncratic to them. We would certainly do it differently! Church and school do not provide much guidance. The Catholic Church once required Pre-Cana (pre-marital) courses for couples about to be married, but they no longer do. The other mass media, especially many women's magazines, occasionally offer much valuable information, but we spend much less time with them than we do with television. Besides, many men never see them and most men's magazines offer very little information.

So, what are we left with? Television. We watch stories about beautiful homes, white picket fences, kids who don't need braces, and spouses who never wake up crabby, have bad breath, look lousy, or fail to resolve problems. And the pictures of marriage that we get from these programs may well influence how we negotiate our own marriages.

Two Michigan State researchers, Judith Walters and Vernon Stone, for example, interviewed seventy-six housewives and asked them questions about their television watching. One third of the people that they talked to said that television watching was a good chance for husband and wife to do something together, but more important, half of the women said that the programs gave them something to talk about. In other words, there are a lot of husbands and wives talking about and discussing what they see on the screen. If much of what they are watching presents a certain picture of marriage and family life, a picture that is inaccurate or stereotyped, it may hurt their evaluation of their own marriage and family life.

My own research suggests that these television presentations of marriage and family do indeed influence how we perceive our own marriage and family experiences. With my colleague, John Courtright of the Cleveland State University, I undertook an investigation of how married and divorced people judged television marriages and how their own marriage experiences measured up against those on the tube. Through the use of a questionnaire designed to get at these issues, we collected information from 119 people. Our findings were then reported to the annual convention of the International Communication Association in May, 1980, in Acapulco, Mexico.

The results clearly showed that a relationship does exist between people's perceptions of television marriages and their satisfaction in their own marriages. We asked people how happy they were in their marriages and whether or not their marriages met the expectations that they had for them before they got married. As you might expect, satisfaction was strongly related to the degree to which their expectations were met.

We also asked people to tell us if they felt that most television marriages were better and/or happier than their own real marriages. Those who responded yes were most likely to be dissatisfied in their own marriages. That is, people who saw television marriages as better than their own (and therefore possibly having higher expectations) were most likely to report less marital satisfaction (possibly because their television-created expectations were not met).

One logical other way to interpret this is to say that people who were less happy in their marriages might see the television marriages as better than their own simply because those video marriages were indeed better. But we conducted an additional analysis that supports the original interpretation of unmet expectations leading to less satisfaction.

We asked the people to name their five favorite television programs and we then paid a graduate student who did not know about the study's purpose to judge the programs that each person had named as either family oriented (portraying marriage and/or family situations) or non-family oriented (not portraying those situations). "All in the Family" would be one example of the former; "Sixty Minutes" and "Charlie's Angels" would be examples of the latter.

What we discovered was that people who identified fewer family oriented shows as favorites had more positive perceptions of their own marriages. That is, the people who named the fewest programs that depicted marriage and family situations seemed to be more happily married—at least they thought they were.

This study is not really "proof" that watching television and liking programs that present marriages and families will result in your divorce and unhappiness. What it did do was show that a relationship exists between watching television marriages and perceiving them in certain ways, and what we come to expect out of our own marriages.

How well we negotiate our own marriages depends in large part on what we expect from them. How we perceive marriage—that is, how we frame it—depends on the quality and type of information we have about it. If we depend on television for that information—either by choice or because there are few other alternatives—we may be using inadequate information to frame and therefore deal with that very important legal, social, moral, and sometimes religious commitment.

The second half of the 1979-80 television season offered us the opportunity to decide for ourselves if we were willing to accept realistic portrayals of marriage and family on television. In March of that season, NBC unveiled "United States," its "realistic" prime-time comedy. Written by Larry Gelbart, who was so successful in writing "M*A*S*H," this new program examined modern marriage and family. CBS's television critic, Jeff Greenfield, called it an "acquired taste" program. That is, because it was unlike other television comedies about families—it had no laugh track, it did have realistic, often painfully accurate portrayals of feelings and emotions—he felt that viewers would be slow in warming up to it.

Diane Holloway, television critic for a small town newspaper, the Austin *American-Statesman,* put it differently. She wrote, "Gelbart's scripts have captured superbly the everyday routines and banter of ordinary married life. Arguments are petty and circular, sentences and thoughts are left dangling most of the time and kids are all-consuming. It is realistic to the point of tedium."

Television finally offered us portrayals of marriage and family that are realistic and one critic—a fan— worries about its success and another—a foe—calls it tedious because it "captured superbly" the essence of marriage. Where did you stand? Which were you willing to do? Would you watch the Nelson family, and occasionally wonder what Ozzie did for a living? Or would you prefer to watch Richard and Libby Chapin, united in a realistically portrayed state of matrimony, and be forced to reflect on your own marriage and family? Apparently more folks preferred the Nelsons, they had a 14-year network run. "United States" finished dead last in the ratings with its first two episodes and quickly disappeared from the screen.

For years, television programs about families portrayed the way we act and respond in simple, routine, unrealistic ways. We accepted those pictures because that was what we expected from television—and we rarely thought about the consequences. How we react to a different kind of family television show, "United States" for example, can tell us a lot about ourselves as viewers. It can tell us how much we are willing to let television challenge us.

SUGGESTED ADDITIONAL READINGS

Baran, S. J. and Courtright, J. A. "Television Portrayals of Marriage as they Affect Married and Divorced People's Satisfaction in Marriage." *International Communication Association Annual Convention, Acapulco, 1980.*

CHAPTER 7

SHOULD MARSHALL DILLON HAVE SHOT THAT MAN OR SHOULD HE HAVE STRUNG HIM UP?

TELEVISION AND AGGRESSION

And so it is with child molesters. If you do it during the week on the school playground to one child, you are driven off to prison in a police car. But if you do it Saturday morning in the living room to millions of young children you are just driven home by a chauffeur in a long black limousine . . . Private tort actions ought to be very seriously considered by parents and by the victims of violent actions naming the (television) networks as defendants.

> —Former F.C.C. Commissioner Nicholas Johnson in testimony before the U.S. Senate Hearings on the *Surgeon General's Report on Television and Social Behavior,* 1972.

Should Marshall Dillon Have Shot That Man?

Few people have taken Commissioner Johnson's suggestion very seriously, but most of us have, at one time or another, been concerned with television violence. Even if we are unconvinced about the relationship between television violence and subsequent viewer aggression, there has been enough attention directed at the issue to have caused us to wonder just what the relationship might be.

There are a number of reasons why the television violence issue has received so much attention. For one thing, there was a several year period in the 1970's when the amount of violence on television grew tremendously. There was so much televised mayhem, in fact, that one study estimated that average American children were seeing the televised assault or destruction of over 1800 human beings before they reached eighteen years of age. In 1976, for example, 74.9 percent of all television characters presented in network programming in one sample week were involved in violence of some form or other. Nine out of every ten network programs in that sample week contained some violence and there were 6.2 violent acts per network program.

Coupled with this presence of large amounts of violence on television, our society was experiencing increased amounts of violence in the real world, and a lot of blame was laid on television. At the Charles Manson trial, Leslie Van Houten and Brenda McCann blamed "Combat" and "Gunsmoke" for making them take part in the Sharon Tate murders. Television was accused of creating the climate for and then perpetuating the racial and political violence of the late 1960's and early 1970's. The National Commission on the Causes and Prevention of Violence that was established to examine that chaos devoted much of its attention to television violence. The 1977 Ronney Zamora trial in Florida and that state's decision to allow the broadcast of those proceedings brought the story of a nine-year-old boy who killed an elderly lady into our homes. His lawyer and psychiatrists argued that

68

he was innocent by virtue of insanity because he could not distinguish between reality and television; he was not robbing that woman, he was playing out "Kojak."

The 1977 *Born Innocent* trial in California had much of the same impact. The adolescents who raped a nine-year-old girl with a toilet plunger attempted to use television violence as a defense; they claimed that they were inspired by NBC's presentation of *Born Innocent*, a movie depicting a very similar occurrence.

There are many television observers and critics who will even blame those annoying and time-consuming airport security procedures on televised portrayals of violence. Before NBC's December 13, 1966 broadcast of the movie *The Doomsday Flight,* there had been very few incidents of bomb threats against domestic airlines. However, while the film was being aired, one bomb threat was called in to an airline, four more were made the next day, and eight more were made by the end of the seven day period following the broadcast. That was an 800 percent increase in bomb threats over the previous month. Soon after, we began to see increased airport security.

All of this could be relatively easy to ignore. It is so distant, so removed from how we live. And maybe the network people are right, maybe the people who did these things were "predisposed" to violence, they probably weren't normal, well-adjusted individuals like most of the rest of us. But we do see our kids acting out the slow- motion karate and judo moves of "Kung Fu." The "noogies," eye poking, and nose pulling that are standard occurrences on "The Three Stooges" seem to show up in the behavior of good, regular kids. In other words, most of us see enough evidence in our own environments to make us wonder whether television is as innocent as many people claim.

So, the question is, "Does television violence lead to viewer aggression?" The answer is simple, "It depends." This is not a brief restatement of the classic cop-out response, "Some television violence effects some people some times in some ways." That inarguable statement has often been interpreted to mean that some rare presentation of television violence effects some rare, probably predisposed people on some very rare occurrences in relatively minor ways.

This "It depends," on the other hand, means just that—it depends. If we mean does television violence usually lead to direct, observable viewer aggression, the answer is usually no. Of course, there are those rare instances when someone will emulate what he or she has seen on television and engage in some aggressive act that is directly attributable to television, but these events are rare. Most of us do not pack .38's, we cannot administer slow-motion doses of kung fu to people who annoy us. We do not usually jump off roofs onto unsuspecting criminals, and bank robbery, high-jacking, drug smuggling, and murder are not usual parts of our daily routine.

This point is one of the reasons that there is so much dispute about the effects of televised violence. Even with the presence of so much media mayhem, very few people actually appear to be influenced. It is true, they may not seem to be influenced—not if we define influence as direct, observable emulations of what was on the screen.

Remember we talked about the Burt Reynold's movie, *Fuzz,* in Chapter 1? It was the one in which a group of punks burned a derelict to death after dousing him in gasoline. Within a week after it aired on television, two remarkably similar murders were carried out. The cry went up, "See, television violence leads to viewer aggression!" "No way," countered television industry spokespeople, "Millions and millions of viewers saw the movie and only a very few, no doubt crazy people who were predisposed to violence in the first place did those regrettable things."

It's tough to argue with that logic. Why should television be blamed for the misdeeds of a handful of unbalanced individuals? Why should all the audience suffer because a few people are adversely influenced? If it was only these unbalanced few that were susceptible to the influence of televised violence, we could easily dismiss the problem as a mountain constructed from a mole hill. But we may all be being influenced in ways that are much more subtle and possibly more destructive.

There was a cartoon in the newspaper several years ago. A father and son were sitting in front of the television set, apparently watching a western. The boy turned to his father and said, "That guy shouldn't have ridden into town and shot all those people." The next frame of the strip showed the father beaming with pride. No sir, television violence doesn't affect his kid, he raised his son right. In the last frame, however, the son finished his thought, "He should have poisoned the water supply."

There was no direct, observable consequence of watching that desperado ride into town and gun down those folks. The son did not get a gun and shoot anybody. But was he affected? What did he learn about solving problems? About dealing with other people? About the value of human life? What information did he take away from the set that he might later frame some real world experience and how might that framing influence his behavior? That's the reason the answer to the television violence question is, "It depends." We may not be able to see or measure the medium's impact, but it may well be there.

Distinguishing between imitating what's on the screen and identifying with what's on the screen can make it easier to understand the elusiveness of television effects.

Imitation, as we have already discussed, is the direct copying of something that we see. The Fonz leans backwards, cocks his head, thrusts his thumbs toward the rear, and intones, "Aaaaaay" when challenged. Spiderman points his palm at an opponent, presses a button on his hand and ensnares that aggressor in spider's webbing.

71

Should Marshall Dillon Have Shot That Man?

We have all seen children imitate these television actors, just as we have seen adults imitate certain styles of dress, hair, speech, and so on. How many of us can honestly say that we have never heard anyone toast another person with, "Here's looking at you, kid"? That salutation, by the way, is pure Humphrey Bogart, not original with our friend.

Imitation is usually harmless or innocuous. There are occasions, however, when it can be a problem. The two people who were burned to death after the airing of *Fuzz* might agree, as would those airlines that became targets for bomb threats, extortions, and highjackings. Many parents whose children inflict "Three Stooges" punishments on one another might also concur. But the truth is, given all of the programming that is on television, and given all of the watching that we do, these incidents of imitation— while sometimes very serious—are not so frequent that they cannot be dismissed as the play of children, the pleasant adoption of new styles, or the work of lunatics who were probably predisposed to that kind of behavior anyway.

Identification from television, on the other hand, is where our concern should rest. As we have already seen, it is a special kind of imitation, one in which specific, discrete acts are not copied, but one in which the viewer wants to be and tries to be like the characters with regard to their broader qualities. Sometimes this identification is conscious, sometimes it is unconscious. We may not imitate Fonzie's "aaaaaay," but we may identify with and adopt his general style of dealing with people. We may not be able to jump through the air in slow motion to deliver a kung-fu kick to an assailant like Kane does, but we can identify with his mode of problem solving—aggression.

Very few of us would have gone out and burned a wino after seeing *Fuzz*. We simply do not imitate much of what we see on television. But what might watching that program and the countless others that depict the destruction of human beings by other human beings do to us? At what point will we, even though unwilling to imitate those acts, come to identify with the characters' ways of problem solving, their ways of dealing with other people, and their evaluation of the worth of human life?

One standard argument against the operation of this identification is, "There's always been violence; it's even in the Bible and in literature." That's true. But people do not read for seven hours a day, day after day, night after night. The stories in the Bible and in literature were not presented in color, with music, and with fast-paced, exciting editing that encourages identification and involvement.

Albert Bandura, former President of the American Psychological Association and a professor at Stanford University, has explained this imitation of and identification with television violence in terms of his social learning theory of aggression. He argued that the aversive or problem situations that we encounter produce an emotional arousal that calls for action. The behaviors that we call upon to use in solving those problems or dealing with those aversive situations are a function of what we have come to learn for dealing with those situations.

There are a lot of ways to deal with aversive or problem situations. Bandura listed several: dependency (asking for help), achievement ("I will overcome"), withdrawal and resignation, aggression, psychosomaticization ("What problem?"), self-anaesthetization (taking drugs and alcohol), and constructive problem solving. When confronted by a problem situation, our selection of a given behavior is dependent on what we have learned and how effective we see it as being in that situation. Because many of the problems in television shows are solved through aggression, it is easy for us to learn aggression as a problem-solving device or as a way to deal with aversive situations. We may choose to imitate a specific aggressive behavior or identify with a general class of behaviors—

aggression. It depends on what we have learned. In our terms, it depends on how we have come to frame the problem and its solution.

There are a number of ways in which this imitation and identification from television can have effects. One is observational learning—people can learn behaviors simply by seeing them performed. Many of us (and our children) who grew up watching "The Three Stooges" learned the two-fingered eye poke and the defense against that tactic. No one ever formally taught us that putting our hand in salute down the bridge of our nose would ward off the two-finger eye poke, but we saw Curly use it to protect himself from Moe.

There is a good deal of research evidence that documents viewers' ability to observationally learn televised violence. In one such study, children were shown a film that depicted a young child beating up on a large plastic doll while yelling nonsense words like "wetsosmacko." Another similar group of children saw no such film. When put in a room full of toys, the children who had seen the doll-beating were much more likely to beat the doll than were those children who did not see the film, and many even yelled those strange, meaningless words. They had observationally learned aggression.

Another way that we learn from television is through disinhibitory effects. We see television characters engage in actions that we think are prohibited or that are threatening to us and we see them suffer no punishment or sometimes we even see them rewarded. The viewing of these situations can disinhibit—reduce our inhibitions toward—similar actions in our own behavior. It is in this way that researchers and clinicians have reduced people's fears and inhibitions toward dogs, snakes, dentists, and other unpleasant things. They showed their programs and films to people who had inhibitions toward these offending agents. Those program materials depicted characters who suffered no ill effects from snakes, dogs, and dentists.

In the same way, the presentation of televised violence can reduce inhibitions toward real life violence. We see so many robberies, beatings, knifings, and shootings every night that either go unpunished or that are administered in the name of the law that we may begin to lose our inhibitions toward such aggression.

In 1975, for example, a 71-year-old Seattle, Washington refrigerator repairman, no child, robbed a bank, and when asked why he did it, he said that because he had seen so many media robberies, he felt certain that he could get away with it. There is a good deal of scientific research, too, that supports the argument that disinhibition toward real life aggression can result from watching television aggression.

In an experiment similar to the one mentioned above, young children were shown a program in which two small boys were playing but subsequently began fighting. One of the boys—the bully—was rewarded with soda and cookies for beating up the other boy. Another group of children saw the same program, but did not see the rewards given to the bully; they saw him punished. When they were allowed a play period, those kids who saw the bully rewarded engaged in much more aggressive play than did those who saw the punishment. Both groups of kids had seen the violence, but those who saw it rewarded showed more aggression; they had been disinhibited.

That makes sense, you might say, but the kids who saw the bully get his just deserves acted less aggressively. On real television the bad guy always gets punished, so wouldn't the viewers be less likely to act aggressively after they see this. That's a good argument—seeing those bad guys get punished does inhibit aggression, but possibly only temporarily.

Several weeks after the experiment was first run, the researchers returned and offered cookies and soda to the inhibited kids—those who had seen the bully punished—if they could imitate what they had seen on the screen in that program. Almost every child could. Even though the aggression had been inhibited because the kids saw the bully punished, they still learned the behaviors. When there was enough reward or incentive present in the real world, however, they ignored those inhibitions and made the behaviors that they had observationally learned.

We know, for example, that it's stupid to tail-gate another car and flash our high beam headlights in the driver's eyes. We have seen enough media and real life accidents to know that that kind of reckless driving is senseless. But when some clown cuts us off on the highway, or will not let us into the lane of traffic that we need to be in, we may forget that inhibition and get on that turkey's tail. By the same token, we all know the potential outcome of a fist fight—black eye, bloody nose, pain— but there are times that the real world environment demands that we ignore those inhibitions and fight an offender.

The bad-guy-always-gets-punished argument is faulty for two other reasons. In the case of most young children, they cannot relate the punishment that the villain receives at the end of the program to the violent or aggressive action that he or she made at the beginning of the show. The other problem centers on the mode of punishment. How are bad guys usually punished? They are out-drawn, out-wrestled, out-shot, out-fought, or in other words, out-aggressed by the hero. So we may have villains punished for their violence, but we also have heroes rewarded for theirs.

Consider a small child, then. He or she may see the bad guy beat someone up in the first five minutes of a show and then the villain is beaten up in the last five minutes. This may not be seen as a bad person getting his or her just rewards; it is probably perceived as two pretty exciting fights.

76

The bad-guy-always-gets-punished defense of television violence is not the only one that is offered to counter the television violence-leads-to-viewer-violence claim. Another is the "it's-only-fantasy" claim. In effect, it contends that everyone knows that it's only television; it's fake, and because it's fake, it has no effect. A group of researchers put this argument to the test. They concocted an experiment where a man escorted young children to a play room in their school. As he took each child individually down the hall to the room, another man walked by and they bumped into one another. A fight broke out while the child watched. After the fight, the child was allowed to use the play room.

A second set of children experienced the same treatment, but there was no second man or fight in the hall. When they came upon the play room, however, the experimenter announced that there was someone in it and they would have to watch television for a little while.

The set was hooked up to a videotape machine and when the experimenter turned it on, there was a program about two men who bump into each other and then have a fight. Another set of kids went through the same procedure, but the people who had the fight on television were dressed in animal costumes and were on a stage that was decorated with cardboard trees and so on.

Each child was then given time in the play room, and those children who had seen the most unrealistic violence—the last condition—engaged in the most aggressive play. So much for the it's-only-fantasy argument. The more real the violence the less likely are we to identify with it. The real fight in the hall, for example, was accompanied by the sound of blows, grunts, groans, and pain. The costumed combatants were using violence that was perceived as funny or as a joke.

Two other related arguments are the "we-don't-show-the-details" and the "it's-always-part-of-the-plot-never-unnecessary-violence" claims. On the surface, these seem

77

like reasonable arguments. Television does avoid the graphic details of violence and it rarely presents mindless, unjustified violence. In fact, the National Association of Broadcasters' Television Code tells stations and networks that, "Violence, physical or psychological, may only be projected in reasonably handled contexts, not used exploitatively. Programs involving violence for its own sake and the detailed dwelling upon brutality or physical agony, by sight or by sound, are not permissible." Reasonable enough, or so it would seem.

But each defense is flawed. Television effects research has demonstrated that presenting violence in the absence of its ugly consequences, like the fantasy violence already discussed, promotes subsequent viewer aggression. The viewer learns the act—hitting with a two-by-four, knifing, shooting—without learning the consequences—bashed and bleeding heads, ugly bleeding cuts, chunks of flesh torn away. In fact, the best way to show violence is to show its consequences, show the agony and suffering, show the real world consequences. What is television telling kids about guns when Moe shoots Curley in the bottom with a shot gun and Curley runs and puts his tail in a rain barrel to the sound of hissing steam, emerging unhurt? It tells them that guns are funny, that they don't kill.

There is also a wealth of scientific evidence that questions the justifiable violence defense. When violence is presented on television as reasonable and justifiable, viewers learn not only the behavior, but they learn that these are good, useful, justifiable behaviors. The prohibition against violence for its own sake leads to the presentation of justified violence and justified violence may lead to increased aggression. In fact, in several studies just that relationship was demonstrated. Giving a reason for violence provides it with a context, it makes it easier to use in the real world, it makes it easier to frame.

There are two other areas of television violence

research that have just begun to receive public attention. Each deals with effects that are difficult to document and each suggests the kind of effects that most of us do not like to think about.

One of those areas deals with the way we frame our real world based on information that we learn from television. Take a minute and answer these three questions. They were developed by George Gerbner and his colleagues at the Annenberg School of Communication for their annual Television Violence Profile conducted for the National Institute of Mental Health:

1. During a given week, what are the chances that you will be involved in some kind of violence?
a. less than 1 in 100   b. about 1 in 10   c. about 3 in 10

2. What percent of all working males are involved in law enforcement and/or crime detection?
a. 1%   b. 5%   c. 10%

3. What percent of all crimes are violent crimes (murder, rape, robbery, aggravated assault)?
a. 10%   b. 15%   c. 20%

The answers are a. (.41 violent crimes per 100 people according to police data), a. (1% according to the 1970 U.S. Census), and a. (10% according to the U.S. Statistical Abstract). How did you fare? Did you consistently choose an answer that was higher than the correct (that is, real world) answer?

Most people do and one reason may be that they are making judgments about the real world based on television-provided information. On television there are a lot of cops, private eyes, criminals, and crime. What happens when we begin to see our real world as being populated in the same way?

One thing that may happen is that we may alter how we deal with the real world. We may be unwilling to go downtown at night because of the "crime." When we stop going downtown, businesses close, and crime moves in. It becomes a self-fulfilling prophecy.

We may begin to mistrust our neighbors, particularly if they are non-white or foreign (a very large proportion of television heavies are either non-white or foreign).

You may remember Plato's fable of the cave. He told Glaucon of a race of people who had been chained in a cave and the only thing that they could see other than themselves were the shadows that their fire cast upon the cave's walls. They thought that the outside world was populated by these frightening monsters because they had no way to know that they were only shadows. We may be spending so much time in front of our sets that we start to see the shadows that it casts as real, we may come to see those pictures as reality.

The other area of recent concern with television violence deals with desensitization. This aspect of television impact inquiry has not received much attention because it suggests something about us as individuals that may make us uncomfortable. It argues that we may be becoming desensitized to violence and aggression against other people because we have become so familiar with it from television. The repeated presentation in our homes of killings, rapes, muggings, shootings, car wreckings, knifings, and fighting may be reducing our aversions toward these events in real life.

Two experiments demonstrate how desensitization may occur. In one, a researcher presented students with anthropological films of aboriginal tribespeople engaging in a religious rite in which human genitals were disfigured. The viewers were connected to devices that measured pulse rate and sweating, two physiological signs of emotional upset.

At the first showing of the film, all the viewers showed very strong aversions to what was on the screen. By the sixth showing, they showed no aversion. They had become desensitized to the violence.

So what, you say, those films weren't television and that doesn't mean that they were desensitized to real world aggression. Here, then, is where the second study becomes important.

In this experiment a researcher individually interviewed children to get some judgment of their television preferences. She was able to place the kids on a scale that went, at one end, from preferring violent programming to preferring non-violent programming at the other. She used such things as favorite shows, favorite characters, favorite episodes, and so on to rate the children.

When each interview was complete, she told the child that there was one last page of questions that she needed to ask, but she had left it in her office. She would get it, she said, and return in a moment. There was, she remembered, however, a problem. There was another child in the room next to theirs and he was a little wild. If he knew that she was gone, he might act up. So the woman asked the child to watch the problem boy in the next room for her. She turned on what was supposed to be a closed circuit television that could be used to watch the room in which the supposed problem child was playing. In actuality, it was a monitor connected to a videotape machine and it played the same tape for each of the children in the experiment.

Once the set was turned on, the woman left and each child watched the boy at play in the next room. After a few moments he began acting up, knocking things over, tearing books, and so on.

When the woman returned, she asked the child to report on the behavior of the problem boy. What she discovered was that those children who had high preference for television violence were more likely to report that he had done nothing wrong, while those who had non-violent program preferences tended to report that he had behaved rather badly. Those kids who were heavy television violence users and likers had become desensitized to violence; they saw his actions as unaggressive, as not bad.

Is it true? Are we becoming desensitized? How many of us would hear the accounts of the dead and wounded from Viet Nam and feel good that only 20 men were killed and 80 wounded? The death of one man should have distressed us, but the constant news of war casualties desensitized us; we became accustomed to boys being killed. Is it unreasonable to assume that the nightly array of television killings might have a similar effect on us?

It depends. There are a number of factors that will influence whether we learn violence from television, use that violence in our everyday lives, come to see our world as a violent one, become desensitized to violence and aggression. Each of us is the only one who can know for sure. But Jesse Steinfeld, who was the Surgeon General at the time of the 1972 report of the Surgeon General's Scientific Advisory Committee on Television and Social Behavior, expressed his opinion, "These studies (the *Surgeon General's Report on Television and Social Behavior*)— and scores of similar ones—make it clear to me that the relationship between televised violence and antisocial behavior is sufficiently proved to warrant immediate remedial action. Indeed the time has come to be blunt: We can no longer tolerate the present high level of televised violence that is put before children in American homes."

ADDITIONAL SUGGESTED READINGS

Bandura, A. "Social Learning Theory of Aggression." *Journal of Communication,* 28, 1978, 12-29.

Feshbach, S. and Singer, R. D. *Television and Aggression.* San Francisco: Jossey-Bass, 1971.

Gelles, R. J. *The Violent Home.* Beverly Hills: Sage, 1974.

Milgram, S. and Shotland, R. L. *Television and Antisocial Behavior.* New York: Academic Press, 1973.

CHAPTER 8

IS THAT THE WAY IT IS?

TELEVISION NEWS AND THE REAL WORLD

My overwhelming impression of all those hours in all those years (on the road) is of hair . . . Hair carefully styled and sprayed, hair neatly parted, hair abundant, and every hair in place . . . The plain truth is that in a society which depends on an informed citizenry, and in which most citizens receive most of their information from television, millions are getting that life- giving information from a man—or a woman—whose colleagues wouldn't trust him to accurately report on his afternoon round of golf.

> —Charles Kuralt, CBS "On the Road" reporter in an address to the Radio Television News Directors Association in Dallas in 1975

Is That the Way It Is?

I had the good fortune to meet one of Mr. Kuralt's well-coiffured newscasters and to talk with her about television news. It was at a luncheon in Cleveland, Ohio, where I was the featured speaker. In response to a question from the audience, I said that I felt that the stations in that town were not doing a particularly good job of reporting the news. Sure, I thought that the story in which the "action news reporter" took a lesson in animal taming and was mauled by an uncoopertive lion was O.K. I was even entertained by the report of the last remaining hard Christmas candy factory. But as for covering the events of the day, maybe they could have been doing a little bit better.

"I strongly disagree," shouted a very attractive woman, every hair in place (a dead give away). "I'm tired of hearing all this criticism," she said, "In fact, given that we only have about eleven minutes to report the news, I think that we do a good job." She was a reporter for one of the three major television stations in Cleveland. Her words were greeted with a small smattering of applause.

She was right. Having only eleven minutes to report the news in a half hour broadcast, it is pretty difficult to do good, incisive reporting. But I asked her who it was that limited her news program to one half hour. Why were there only eleven minutes of news in that thirty minutes of air time? Was the time spent on weather and sports necessary? Was the happy talk and friendly banter that was exchanged between the anchor people really necessary? Why were so many of those 30 minutes set aside for commercials? And with everything else happening in the city—not to mention the state, country, and world—that might influence her viewers' lives, why were several of those minutes devoted to a newsman learning to tame a lion and a hard Christmas candy factory that was doing a booming business?

I suggested that she was like a carpenter who tells his boss that he is building the best house that he can, given that all he has to work with is a rubber hammer and a plastic saw. Carpenters are supposed to get the right tools for the job and then use them to their fullest. To say that the stations were doing a good job, given that they had only eleven minutes of news was no defense. They were the ones who limited themselves to eleven minutes, they were the ones who were making inefficient use of their tools.

She had no response. I received a large smattering of applause.

In one sense, however, she was accurate. Local television news is good television—fast-paced, exciting, entertaining. The performers are friendly and attractive. It is such good television, in fact, that 40 to 60 percent of most television stations' profits come from their nightly local news programs. Local news shows have become so lucrative, that most stations hire "news doctors," specialists in improving the ratings of news shows, to help spice up those broadcasts in order to draw more viewers which means higher ratings which results in even more profits.

The news doctors prescribe such practices as reporting a large number of different stories, keeping them very short. Stations are instructed to use a lot of visual materials, even if they are not necessary. That's why we often see a picture of a smoking gun or the word "murder" over the anchorperson's shoulder while they read a report of a killing, for example. The news doctors stress a team atmosphere for the local news show. It conveys a sense of warmth and friendliness; the anchors and reporters are nice, honest people, they are our pals. The doctors also prescribe very simple stories, and they tell their clients to stay away from too much detail. Too boring, they say.

This medicine usually results in healthy ratings. But good entertainment, healthy ratings, and profitable television do not necessarily mean good news.

These practices leave very little room for detailed,

85

thorough reporting. There is no depth or analysis. Stories tend to be chosen for their visual as opposed to informational value. The half hour quickly begins to shrink to those eleven minutes as the weather girl and the sports reporters talk about their respective tomato gardens.

Why should we be concerned about the quality of this news? After all, we are getting some information, and it's pleasantly and interestingly packaged. For one thing, as Charles Kuralt said, the proper function of our own society is based on the presence of an informed citizenry. A democracy demands that the people make reasoned decisions. How informed are we, however, when we get our information from several pleasantly packaged, fast-paced, short segments tucked into eleven minutes a night? Not much you say, but the truth is, most of us are content to get most of our information from these programs. A 1979 Roper Organization survey commissioned by the Television Information Office discovered that sixty-seven percent of us get "most of our news about what's going on in the world today" from television. Forty-seven percent of the respondents said that television was their most believable source of news.

With that many people dependent on television for their world view, it seems like television news should be less concerned with hair and entertainment and more concerned with information.

A second reason that we should be concerned with the performance of our local news programs is that these shows help us frame the everyday situations that we encounter. Remember in the last chapter when you were asked what percent of crime in this country is violent crime? Think about your answer in terms of the way crime is presented on the local news shows. White collar crime is not visual and fast-paced—no police sirens screaming, no bodies in the street, no bullet holes in the wall. Robberies, murders, drug busts, and rapes are very visual and fast-paced—police sirens screaming, bodies in the street, bullet holes in the wall. Many of those nightly eleven news minutes go to robberies, murders, drug busts, and rapes. Much of our world view comes from these images on the screen.

Sure, we know better. We know that there is a whole wider world out there than the one those eleven minutes tell us about. But why did most of us answer the question about violent crimes incorrectly? Why then are 67 percent of us willing to get most of our news from television and why do 47 percent of us see it as the most believable medium?

One of the reasons is that the stations encourage us to take their reports as complete, accurate accountings of the day's events. They give their news programs names like "Eyewitness News" and "Action News" and they tell us about their "on the spot coverage," all designed to make us believe that what we are seeing is the way it is.

But there are dramatic differences between an event and what is reported about that event. We are hardly eyewitnesses, we are not near the action, and we are far removed from on the spot. For example, a reporter covers the story in a certain way; the cameraperson shoots it according to his or her own set of professional, technical, and personal criteria; back at the station, a writer produces the copy for the anchor-person and voice-over announcer to read on the air; the film editor cuts and splices the film based on the available footage and selection of shots; the news director decides how much time the story should get, where it should be placed in the program, and what other visuals might be used.

· These professionals are necessary and important agents in the newsgathering and news dissemination process. We need them to get the news and deliver it to us. But we cannot allow ourselves to believe that their product is always or even usually complete and accurate. When we watch their news shows, we are watching television representations of the way it is, we are not eyewitnesses.

There are some encouraging signs, however, on the local news scene. The "happy talk" format seems to be giving way in many news shows to a format that stresses structured, professional informality. This reintroduction of journalism into local news is the result of a number of factors.

Television's role in the Watergate scandals and successful network news programs like the three networks' nightly news shows and "Sixty Minutes" have raised viewers' expectations of their own local news operations. And expectations have to be met if ratings are to be maintained.

This has led in some markets to things like post-news magazine shows—expanded "soft news" programs that follow the regular news—freeing the station to use its eleven minutes for "hard news." Some stations have gone to an hour or an hour and a half of local news. A few have even created their own investigative reporting team, a' la "Sixty Minutes."

If you live in a major market, you may be familiar with some of these innovations. We should be encouraged by the increased reporting and proud that it was our implicit demand for better news that brought them about. But many of us live in small media markets where this new breed of television news show is still rare.

The problem is money. According to *Broadcasting,* the television industry bible, a television station news operation in one of the top ten media markets can make between two and six million dollars a year on its evening local news show. Stations in the eleventh to twentieth markets make between one and three million dollars from news. Smaller market stations make smaller amounts of money.

A station in a bigger market can turn much more money back into its news operation than a smaller market station can. No matter what size the market is, cameras, videotape, film, and all the other things necessary to produce a news show still cost the same. Richer stations can afford to innovate, other stations cannot. So most of us outside of the major markets, then, and even many of us in them, are still getting hair . . . hair carefully styled and sprayed, hair neatly parted, hair abundant, and every hair in place.

SUGGESTED ADDITIONAL READINGS

Cirino, R. *Don't Blame the People*. New York: Random House, 1972.

Cirino, R. *Power to Persuade; Mass Media and the News*. New York: Bantam Books, 1974.

Crouse, T. *The Boys on the Bus*. New York: Ballantine, 1974.

Diamond, E. *Good News, Bad News*. Cambridge, Mass.: M.I.T. Press, 1978.

Efron, E. *The News Twisters*. Los Angeles: Nash Publishing, 1971.

Gans, H. J. *Deciding What's News*. New York: Free Press, 1979.

Hohenberg, J. *The News Media: a Journalist Looks at His Profession*. New York: Holt, Rinehart and Winston, 1968.

Powers, R. "Eyewitless News." *Columbia Journalism Review,* 1977, 16, 17-24.

Schlesinger, P. *Putting Reality Together: B.B.C. News*. London: Constable and Company, 1978.

Schudson, M. *Discovering the News: a Social History of American Newspapers*. New York: Basic Books, 1978.

Tuchman, G. *Making News: a Study in the Construction of Reality*. New York: Free Press, 1978.

CHAPTER 9

IF ONE IS BORN EVERY MINUTE
AND I WAS BORN,
AM I ONE?

COMMERCIALS

Since most of the products aren't special, most advertising does all that so-called image stuff, which is bullshit. There's no information about the product, there's only information about the kind of people who might be inclined to *use* the product. Which, to me, is dishonest.

> —Former advertising executive, Robert Pritikin, on contemporary advertising. From "Charlie Haas on Advertising," *New West,* November 5, 1979.

If One Is Born Every Minute, Am I One?

For a former ad industry insider, Mr. Pritikin doesn't like contemporary commercials very much. But somebody sure does. Over six billion dollars is spent every year by advertisers who are anxious to get word of their product before the television audience. That amount doesn't include the cost of making the commercials, that's just what they pay the networks and local stations to air them. The three television networks alone take in over three billion dollars in sales of their time every year.

Proctor and Gamble annually spends nearly 400 million dollars on television to tell us that Pampers absorb more, that Crest kills the cavity creeps, and their other products are the best. General Foods puts up over 200 million dollars a year to buy half minutes to tell us about Minute Rice and their other products, like Maxwell House Coffee and Good Seasons Salad Dressing. Ma Bell, who we would think had little need to push her telephone, shells our nearly 60 million dollars, and even McDonalds spends about 100 million dollars to buy thousands of commercial breaks every year to tell us about the hamburger breaks that we deserve today.

All of this money is spent because television commercials sell products. Many of us may even welcome the information about products that they provide, the choices that they make us aware of, the fact that they can tell us about new products. A lot of us may even enjoy them as good television: the Alka-Seltzer "I can't believe I ate the whole thing" ads were entertainment genius, and Pepsi and Coke commercials are splashes of fetching color, action, and music.

Why, then, have television commercials received so much criticism? Sure, there sometimes appears to be too many. It's true, they often come at very inopportune points in the program. And you're right, they very often are loud and offensive. But there is another reason that these television spots attract so much adverse attention—

92

they may be selling us more than products, they may be doing something besides informing.

Take the Wisk "Ring around the Collar" campaign. In each ad, someone sees that the husband has dirt on the inside of his shirt collar and then sings out, "Ring around the collar." The guy is mortified and he looks at his wife in disgust. She has failed him and subjected him to ridicule. She buys Wisk and . . . no more ring around the collar. The husband and wife hug and all is well.

After watching one of these ads, what information do we now have about Wisk? Not too much, but we know that a man's cleanliness and public appearance are his wife's responsibility. We know that she is a failure as a wife if he is unclean. We know that men evaluate their wives based on such matters as ring around the collar, not on more significant matters such as love, tenderness, ability to raise a family, consideration, and so on. And we learn that the way to restore harmony in a marriage is to buy and use products—in this case Wisk.

There are hundreds of similar examples. How do we get the good life? Buy Lancer's wine, of course. How do we get people to like us? Wear Haggar slacks, brush our teeth with Ultra-Brite, drink diet soda, use Lady Clairol, roll on Mennen deodorant, and flick each others Bics.

What makes a good mother? Using Downy because it keeps baby's diaper both soft *and* white. It has nothing to do with conceiving children and bearing them for nine months, giving birth to them and feeding and tending to them for endless hours every day and night. It has nothing to do with loving them and sacrificing for them.

What makes a good father? Buying a piece of the rock to protect your children when you're gone, of course. The fact that you conceive, tend to, nurture, and love your children doesn't mean too much; that you've bought a product that gives them protection after you're dead is what matters.

Remember the little example from Chapter 1? Someone comes up to you in a bar and asks if you'd like a drink. You immediately check him or her out, make judgments about his or her intentions, try to figure out the approach being used. What we do in these situations is pay very close attention to the communication that is occurring. Nowhere in television communication is this scrutiny more necessary than in commercials.

The Federal Trade Commission implicitly realizes this with its rules against false advertising. The FTC acknowledges that people need protection and their sanctions against commercials that lie outright, do not tell the whole truth, or lie by implication using "statement, word, design, device, sound, or any combination thereof" are designed to give us a chance at accurate evaluation and interpretation of these messages.

In the first instance, outright misstatements of fact, the FTC has some leverage. All they had to do was ask Wonder Bread to name the 12 ways that their product builds strong bodies. The Wonder Bread folks couldn't. All they had to do was ask the Listerine people to prove that their mouth wash killed cold germs. They couldn't.

The Commission can also require that advertisers tell the whole story. They have required certain drug and medicine sponsors to make announcements, either written or oral, that drowsiness may occur with use of the product. Other advertisers must report that batteries are not included, or that assembly is required.

But it is in the last area of false advertising, lying by implication, that problems arise. The FTC has caught some violators. Profile Bread used to be advertised as a "diet bread." In fact, the commercials would announce, each slice had only half the calories of a regular slice of bread. That was a true statement, but each slice had half the calories because it was half the size. Equal amounts of Profile Bread and another bread had the same number of calories, Profile was just cut into thinner slices. The implication that it was a diet bread was obviously false.

The Campbell Soup commercials that showed a lot of noodles, vegetables, and beef poking through the broth were deemed false because the advertisers had poured glass marbles into the bowl and, as the heavy glass sank to the bottom, the noodles, vegetables, and beef were forced to the top. The implication that a bowl of Campbell's soup had all that food-stuff was clearly false.

But what about the implication that use of a product can alter your life or improve your lifestyle? That is being communicated in the Ultra-Brite ads, for example? The guy can't get this girl to pay any attention to him so he wants to buy a new sweater to get her to notice him. His pal says, "Put your money where your mouth is," use Ultra-Brite. He does. In the next scene the lovelorn guy has the girl. The implication is clear, buy this product and you will be successful with the opposite sex. The implication in Ultra-Brite's other ads, the ones that have beautiful women saying, "This little tube changed my love life," is equally clear and equally false.

The same can be said for almost every other commercial on television. They imply—through statement, word, design, device, sound, and combinations thereof—that consumption of their product will lead to a better life, happiness, success with the opposite sex, financial security, and the eradication of housetosis, the frizzies, the blahs, and visible panty lines.

These implications are often not very subtle, but the FTC is powerless to confront the sponsors because *we* read those messages into the commercials—or so the sponsors would claim. The fact that we chose to see the guy's success with women as a result of his use of Ultra-Brite is our fault; besides, it doesn't mean that all people will reap the same happiness from that product use. The fact that we interpret the ring around the collar ads to mean that a wife's worth is dependent on her ability to keep her husband's shirts clean through the use of a cleaning product is our fault, the Wisk people never said it.

That's true. Implications are in the mind's eye of the beholder. Advertisers, however, spend millions and millions of dollars every year to insure that their commercials make us see a particular connection between their product and our own everyday life. They do their best to put a certain picture in front of our minds' eyes.

One method of advertising research is the focus group. This is a group session, led by a moderator who is usually a market researcher, that is designed to elicit feelings and opinions about products and commercials. Much deeper information than like/dislike can be elicited from the consumers who are invited to participate—how does the product make you feel, can you identify with the people in the ads, did the music make you feel tingly all over, would your friends like you more if you used this product, and so on.

Face-to-face interviews are another form of advertising research. The same information is gathered by a researcher who sits down individually with people and asks questions, shows pictures of the product and segments from the ads, and so on. These forms of research, however, are seen as too limited by many advertising researchers—all they measure is our rational reaction to the products and their ads.

Other advertising researchers use physiological tools like galvanic skin response meters that measure our level of physical excitation by analyzing how fast an electrical current passes from one electrode to another that are placed on our skin. Voice pitch analysis uses a computer to analyze excitement and tension in consumers' voices as they talk about products and commercials. Still another is the eye-tracking camera, a device that films our eye movements as we watch an ad to measure where we direct our attention. An infrared beam is bounced off a viewer's corneas and is reflected onto a television screen that he or she is watching to indicate where the most attention is being paid.

Another research method is brain wave analysis where viewers are connected by electrodes to computers that analyze their reaction to ads.

All of this research is not designed to create ads that bring us the best and most useful information about a product; it is used to make commercials that influence our emotions, not our intellect. It is used to create commercials that force us to see the emotional implications that will help sell the product.

The advertising industry's newspaper, *Advertising Age,* called this work MESEARCH (all capitals, by the way). They wrote, "Products and services that promise 'me-ness' are fast overtaking products and services that merely promise function." They continued, MESEARCH can help "define the 'me' that is in a brand." The goal is to find ways to present products in commercials so that viewers will see the product and life as synonymous.

So we no longer drink beer; we grab for the gusto. We no longer drink sodas; we join the Pepsi Generation or we may become a Pepper. We no longer enlist in the military; we join the people who join the Army.

A danger exists in these efforts to have us confuse products for life. We may come to use communication about those products (the commercials) to frame our communication in everyday life.

Skeptical? Question 2 in Chapter 1, the one about being a job interviewer and having to choose between two similar candidates, one who drinks Lowenbrau and Heineken and one who favors Bud and Schlitz, how did you answer it? When this choice was offered to experimental subjects (who thought they were actually choosing between real applicants), a majority of the "employers" chose the Lowenbrau/Heineken drinker. Why?

Why is the use of a product part of our evaluation of a person, of ourselves? In other words, why do we frame others and ourselves as advertisers would have us frame others and ourselves?

"Not me," you say, "I know better." Well, have you ever borrowed someone else's car to pick up a date or a friend? Have you ever borrowed someone else's clothes to wear on a date or to an event?

If you answered yes to either of these, think about why. Why are we unwilling to meet someone or present ourselves to someone simply as the best person we can be? Why are we so concerned with the material manifestations of our worth? The reason, as one advertising man was recently quoted, is because, "Not everybody out there (in the real world) is as handsome, wealthy, or well-dressed as those people (in commercials), but don't we all aspire to be something more than we are?"

He is correct, we should "aspire to be something more than we are." But should we so easily accept the advertisers' solution to self-improvement—the purchase of products? Should we so easily accept their definition of self-improvement—better looks, more wealth, finer attire? Whatever became of kindness, generosity, and honesty as measures of a person's worth?

Well, now that you've done such a good job of reading this chapter, go get yourself a Budweiser, after all—this one's for you! Your reward for a job well done is not the respect of your colleagues, self-satisfaction, or the love of your family; it is a product, a good cold beer.

And while you're at it, be a good American, go buy yourself a Chevy. Be a good parent, buy your kids Radio Shack's home computer. Put your family's welfare in good hands, buy more insurance. Don't get older, buy Preference by L'Oreal and get better. And who knows, maybe some day your spouse will say, "I think I'll keep you" because you so wisely took Geritol.

SUGGESTED ADDITIONAL READINGS

Barnouw, E. *The Sponsor: Notes on a Modern Potentate.* New York: Oxford Press, 1978.

Brower C. *Me and Other Advertising Geniuses.* Garden City, N. Y.: Doubleday and Company, 1974.

Buxton, E. *Promise Them Anything.* New York: Stein and Day, 1972.

Della Femina, J. *From Those Wonderful Folks Who Gave You Pearl Harbor.* New York: Simon and Schuster, 1970.

Ogilvy, D. *Confessions of an Advertising Man.* New York: Ballantine, 1963.

Polykoff, S. *Does She . . . or Doesn't She?* Garden City, N.Y.: Doubleday and Company, 1975.

CHAPTER 10

CAN SOMETHING THAT'S SO MUCH FUN BE ALL BAD?

TELEVISION'S GOOD POINTS AND WHAT WE CAN DO TO MAKE THAT NUMBER GROW

(Television) could make of the people of this country so much more than what they are in terms of their capacity to fulfill the potential that they hold, but (it's) not doing it. That's the crime.

—Former F.C.C. Commissioner Nicholas Johnson in testimony before the U.S. Senate Hearings on the Surgeon General's Report on Television and Social Behavior, 1972.

Can Something That's So Much Fun Be All Bad?

Even if we didn't agree with Commissioner Johnson's idea to have criminal charges filed against network executives for "molesting" children with their programming, it is hard to fault his argument here. Very few of us—even the hardest core television fan—will claim that television is doing all that it can in the service of its audience.

But it's a business, some people claim. Why should it serve the public any more than the Ford Motor Company or the local supermarket? It's true, broadcasting is a business, but it is a very special one.

The Radio Act of 1927 declared that the airwaves belong to the people of this country and that they are a public resource that broadcasters can use only with the public's permission. The Communications Act of 1934 was even more precise: broadcasters could use our airwaves if they use them to serve the "public interest, convenience, or necessity." That is, broadcasters are allowed to use the channels that belong to us, but in exchange they must provide us with programming that serves *our* needs as well as their own desire to make profits.

For this reason the "it's a business" argument is faulty. We are providing them—through three-year licenses granted by the Federal Communication commission—with what one Senator called a "gold mine . . . a license to print money." We have a legal right to demand, and they have a legal obligation to provide, programming in the public interest, convenience, or necessity. But that's the problem, too many of us are willing to accept newer movies, funnier comedies, more sports, and prettier detectives as programming in the public interest. In a very true sense the broadcasters are right, we get what we ask for. What we ask for, however, is a function of what we have come to expect from the medium.

If we continue to see television as a source of movies, comedies, sports, and detective shows, all we will ever ask of the broadcasters is better presentations of that programming. But there is a growing wealth of information that tells us that Nicholas Johnson is correct, the medium has a tremendous but sadly-wasted potential to be more than an entertaining plaything. There is a growing body of research that demonstrates that with some minor changes in the way their communications are packaged and prepared, broadcasters can bring us beneficial as well as entertaining television.

The three ways of learning from television that have traditionally received scientific attention—observational learning, inhibitory, and disinhibitory effects—provide a good starting point for looking at television's potential for good and beneficial programming. For a very long time most research attention has centered on the antisocial or negative impact of television programming—the observational learning of aggression and violence, the inhibition of prosocial behaviors, and the disinhibition of forbidden behaviors. This was because most television programming presented models and characters that were aggressive and/or antisocial. The presence and popularity of programs like "Sesame Street," "Family," "Little House on the Prairie," "The Waltons," and so on, however, has begun to turn research attention in the direction of television's good points.

The observational learning of prosocial behavior and socially appropriate norms from television has been well-documented. In one of my own research studies, I showed second and third grade children a television program that depicted prosocial behavior like cleaning up a messy room, wiping spills, and so on. When allowed a play period in a room filled with toys, many of the children straightened up those portions of the room that were messy, even though they thought that no one was watching.

Two researchers, reporting in the 1972 *Surgeon General's Report on Television and Social Behavior,* presented nursery school children with either "Superman"

103

and "Batman" cartoons or with "Misteroger's Neighborhood" over a four-week period. The kids' behavior was measured in school for the following two weeks. The children who had seen the "Misteroger's" programs showed increases in cooperation, nurturance (support of classmates), verbalization of feeling, rule obedience, tolerance of delay, self-control, and task-persistence—all "lessons" from "Misteroger's Neighborhood." The kids who saw "Superman" and "Batman" did not.

In terms of aggression, several social scientists have demonstrated that children who see television characters solve problems in non-aggressive ways will tend to solve their own real world problems with means other than aggression.

Norms and values, too, can be influenced positively by television. Psychologists James Bryan and Nancy Walbek presented elementary school children with either a lecture on the value of giving, a live play about the value of giving, or a television program that showed a child giving money to some less fortunate people. They then had the children play a bowling game that was fixed, so all the kids won the same number of one-cent coupons. The children were then allowed to spend their coupons on themselves or donate them to poor children. Those who had seen the television character give money to poor children donated the most money to the poor.

Dozens of other studies have shown television's ability to influence the level of self-reinforcement that viewers are willing to adopt for a job well done, the types of norms and moral judgments that individuals internalize, and like Bryan and Walbek, the likelihood of altruistic or giving behavior. And in an experiment that I conducted with two colleagues under a grant from the National Association of Braodcasters, we demonstrated the ability of a program like "The Waltons" to increase the likelihood that viewers would use cooperation when confronted with a problem. Kids who saw a video tape of "The Waltons," where the whole family joined together to find a missing child, were significantly more likely to help a woman who had spilled an arm load of books (actually our confederate) than were children who saw a program that depicted characters working independently at a building blocks game.

Put simply, seeing good, giving, cooperating, well- intentioned characters on television can influence viewer behavior every bit as much as can seeing aggressive, mean, violent ones.

The power of television programs to disinhibit previously forbidden or threatening behaviors has been examined largely in terms of violence and antisocial behavior, but as we have already discussed in Chapter 6, television portrayals of people dealing with dogs, snakes, and dentists have been effective in reducing inhibitions toward these perceived evils. There has been additional work, too, that has shown television's potential to reduce social withdrawal in children by offering them portrayals of other children engaged in pleasant, productive play.

In the case of inhibitions, numerous studies have demonstrated the medium's ability to at least temporarily inhibit aggressive or antisocial activity by showing those behaviors being punished. Similar work has shown television's power to inhibit dangerous or deviant action, such as playing with fire.

The research also tells us that we viewers can influence the medium's beneficial effects. As we have already discussed, the power of "interviewers" or "interpreters" has been well documented. By sitting with our children and talking about the programs, characters' motivations and actions, the reality or fantasy of given situations, the persuasive techniques used in commercials, and so on, we can increase possible good effects and decrease possible bad ones.

But we can also be interpreters for ourselves. We agreed that we would question, scrutinize, and evaluate the honey in the bar who wants to buy us a drink. We even agreed, way back in Chapter 1, that we often question our own children's show of affection. We should question, scrutinize, and evaluate the programs, commercials, and messages that we get from television with the same diligence.

Ultimately, then, we are the final determiners of whether television will have effects on us and our children and whether that impact will be positive or negative. This is not a restatement of the standard industry claim that its programming has no effect other than those that people bring on themselves. As we have already discussed, much programming is designed to have very specific effects and much that is not can still have impact.

The putting of responsibility for television's effects at our own feet simply recognizes that that is our best alternative for controlling television's impact. Former Massachusetts Congressman and Chair of the House Communications Subcommittee, Torbert McDonald, once wrote that depending on the broadcasters to control their potentially harmful programming was like "writing a letter to Santa Claus." Whether we take such a cynical view or not, it is clear that changes in programming practices—even in the face of mountains of research that suggest that change is warranted—are not soon forthcoming.

The responsibility, then, rests with us. We have to stop being passive viewers. We should select our programs carefully and watch them and the commercials that they house with the constant awareness that we are being more than entertained.

When we become active, discriminating, and well-informed television viewers, we make that very often pleasant experience more enjoyable and more likely to result in beneficial effects.

SUGGESTED ADDITIONAL READINGS

Baran, S. J., Chase, L. J., and Courtright, J. A. "Television Drama as a Facilitator of Prosocial Behavior: 'The Waltons.'" *Journal of Broadcasting,* 23, 1979, 277-284.

CBS Office of Social Research. *Learning While They Laugh.* New York: Columbia Broadcasting System, 1978.

Liebert, R. M. and Poulos, R. W. "Television as a Moral Teacher." in T. Lickona (ed.), *Man and Morality.* New York: Holt, Rinehart, and Winston, 1976.

Leibert, R. M. and Poulos, R. W. "TV for Kiddies: Truth, Goodness, Beauty—and a Little Bit of Brainwash. *Psychology Today,* November, 1972.

INDEX